STOP FLIPPING STOP RENTING

SELLER FINANCE YOUR WAY TO FINANCIAL FREEDOM

STOP FLIPPING STOP RENTING

SELLER FINANCE YOUR WAY TO FINANCIAL FREEDOM

Michael Arch
and
Erik Saengerhausen

ISBN: 1517790352
ISBN 13: 9781517790356

TABLE OF CONTENTS

Dedication

Erik dedicates this book to his beautiful wife, Brittany, and his two sons, Colton and Parker. Your love and support for me every day inspires me to do my best.

Mike dedicates this book to his amazing wife, Kimberly, and his two daughters, Delaney and Macy. I treasure every moment with all of you. You are the reason that I get up in the morning.

We would both like to dedicate this book to the original group of investors who trusted us enough to start purchasing our real estate notes even before we had much of a track record. A special thanks to Don and Marylou Kersting, Dick Gueringer, Ivan and Diane Estes, and Delos and Diane Finch. You kept the train moving in the most critical phase of our business. We are forever grateful for the trust you placed in us. A special thank you goes out to Mitchell Rocheleau for all of his time energy and creative genius. Your help with the book and website was invaluable to the success of this project.

We would also like to thank our fantastic team, Linda and Lauren Bugosh, Leroy Benavides, Felipe Garcia and Henry Munguia. Henry A.K.A. HUNGRY HANK is a living legend in San Antonio and has sold hundreds of homes. Henry took a leap of faith and quit his long time stable job to become a full time real estate professional with us and has reached an amazing level of success. We are so proud of you Hank!

Mike Arch and family

Erik Saengerhausen and family

Foreword—Dick Gueringer

June 22, 1943–March 23, 2015

Dick Gueringer had planned on writing the foreword to this book but died unexpectedly just prior to this book being completed. Dick was a very close friend and mentor as well as the single largest note buyer in the history of our company.

Dick was always there for us and provided invaluable counsel and guidance while building our company. His selfless attitude and sincere desire for us to succeed was invaluable to our success. Dick always made time for us.

To all of you older men and women with a little gray hair and wrinkles: don't underestimate the positive influence you can have by encouraging someone to go after his or her dreams. God gave you the privilege of living a long life, and sharing your wisdom and experience can help guide someone on the road to success. Make time for someone who needs you.

Mr. Gueringer, we love you and you are sorely missed. Thank you for believing in us even before we believed in ourselves. Rest in peace, dear friend.

Erik Saengerhausen
Mike Arch

"Definiteness of Purpose is the starting point of all achievement. Don't be like a ship at sea without a rudder, powerless and directionless. Decide what you want, find out how to get it, and then take daily action toward achieving your goal. You will get exactly and only what you ask and work for. Make up your mind today what you want and then start today to go after it! Do it now!"

—*Napoleon Hill*

Introduction

We wrote this book to share what we have learned about the real estate business over the past fifteen years. Real estate is absolutely one of the best vehicles to build wealth and create long-term passive streams of income. This is not a get-rich-quick book and we don't claim to have all the answers. What we do know is that the techniques and strategies in this book have helped us build significant wealth. We are talking about not just the mechanics of a real estate transaction but also the attitudes and philosophies that we have developed and refined over the years. Whether you have done hundreds of real estate transactions or you are just getting started, we hope you find the information in this book valuable and would be honored if you make it part of your library.

Our primary business mentor is Mr. Jim Rohn. Jim was not a real estate guru but more of a modern-day business philosopher. Jim has had a huge impact on our lives and helped shape many of our attitudes and philosophies. Jim passed away in 2009, but his audiobooks are still readily available online. Even if you choose not to become a real estate investor, we highly recommend getting your hands on some of Jim Rohn's materials. Jim's philosophies have helped us in all areas of our lives, not just our real estate business. Jim's website is www.jimrohn.com.

One of the main things we learned from Mr. Rohn was to "work harder on yourself than you do on your job." Jim's point is that personal development is one of the best investments you can make. Buying books and taking courses that will improve your skills is money well spent. Jim encouraged people to work full time on their job and part time on their fortune. We want this book to encourage you and equip you to work on your fortune. Congratulations for making a decision to improve your knowledge and skills.

There are many different approaches to building wealth by using real estate. Two of the most common approaches are acquiring rental properties and flipping houses. Both of these strategies just about drove us out of the business. Dealing with tenants, toilets, and vacancies gets old, and flipping houses is definitely not as easy as they make it look on television. The investment strategy taught in this book is seller financing. Seller financing means you are collecting payments from someone who *owns* the house, not someone who *rents* the house. This simple distinction is huge.

If you think becoming a house flipper is your calling, create a real estate note instead, and then "flip" the note. It is a much easier way to sell a home and more profitable once you know how to do it. This book will show you how. If you think getting an 8 percent return on a rental property is good, wait until we show you how to get 16 percent by offering seller-financing terms. If you are going to climb the real estate ladder of success, make sure your ladder is leaning against the right wall—the seller-financing wall.

This book is coauthored by Erik Saengerhausen and Mike Arch. Writing a book alone is hard enough, but try getting two strong-willed people literally on the "same page." It was like pulling teeth at times, but we truly believe that together we have successfully brought our collective wealth strategies to print. Both of us have been entrepreneurs for most of our lives, but it wasn't until we joined forces that our real estate business exploded. We want to share our knowledge and help you build wealth one property at a time. You do not have to win the lottery to make millions of dollars. Just take a systematic approach and focus on one transaction at a time and you are on your way.

Prior to joining forces, Erik and I were each operating independently trying to find the best way to provide for our families. I was making a living flipping a handful of homes each year and day-trading stocks. Erik was a real estate agent and worked for a brokerage company that specialized in selling foreclosed homes and was also flipping a few homes a year. One day, while searching through the Multiple Listing Service, I came across a foreclosure listing that I wanted to see. I called the agent listed on the MLS sheet. It was a crazy German named Erik Saengerhausen. Erik answered the phone "This is the KING of foreclosures, how can I help you?" I told the extremely confident "KING" that I wanted to go take a look at the property and he said that he would meet me there in an hour.

When we met at the property, we spent about five minutes looking at the house and then started talking. About three hours went by and we were still talking about real estate. The next day, we met at a local coffee shop to continue our conversation. We talked about getting rich by flipping houses and how we could join forces to flip on a larger scale. Even though we are both very independent people, we each had a desire to work together because of the synergy and enthusiasm that seemed to flow every time we got together and talked real estate. We started making a huge list of the goals we wanted to achieve and the core philosophies that would guide us.

Here are some of the fundamentals we agreed on from the beginning:

1. **It's about results:** No apologies and no excuses for our results. Look in the mirror and point to the guys in the mirror if things are not going as they should.
2. **Families first**: Don't miss the ballgames and ballet recitals, and make sure we spend quality time with our wives and kids and not become workaholics. Work hard...of course. Workaholics...no way.
3. **Long-term vision**: To build something of value and to build a good reputation, it takes time. We wanted to build our business on honesty and integrity.

4. **Health and fitness**: Make time for health and fitness no matter what! Jim Rohn used to say "Some people don't do well simply because they don't feel well. Take care of your body…it's the only place that you have to live right now."
5. **Spirituality**: We picked out a Bible verse that best articulates the philosophy that we wanted to live by. It is Proverbs 3: 5–6: "Trust in the Lord with all your heart and lean not on your own understanding; in all your ways acknowledge Him and He will make your paths straight."
6. **Discipline**: Jim Rohn used to say, "Everyone suffers one of two pains: discipline or regret. Discipline weighs ounces and regret weighs tons." Building a business and a fortune is hard work. We each committed to discipline ourselves to stay focused every step of the way while building our business. We did not want to regret missing out on our dreams.
7. **Giving back:** We are just stewards of the resources that we have and want to be generous with the fruits of our labor. Giving is one of the greatest joys on earth.

Once we had a meeting of the minds on how we were going to approach the business, it was time to set some lofty goals to help keep us motivated and on track. We decided to set a goal to flip one hundred homes in one year. We needed something to reach for if we were going to accomplish all of our personal goals.

We were just a couple of guys without a lot of money, no college degrees and were working out of our bedrooms. How were we going to come up with enough money to flip one hundred houses a year? How were we going to pull this goal off? Believe. Believe. Believe. That is the first step!

> ***"Whatever the mind can conceive and believe, it can achieve."***
>
> ***—Napoleon Hill***

One of the most influential books we have ever read on achieving success is *Think and Grow Rich* by Napoleon Hill. If you do not own the book, *stop reading* and go out and buy it *now*! It has changed many lives and can change yours too. That book taught us several key things including this: if you think about something often enough, your subconscious mind will take over and you will become what you think about. Did you catch that? *You become what you think about.* Can you picture yourself as a multimillion-dollar real estate investor? If the answer is yes, you are on your way. If the answer is no, the next chapter will help you get there.

Think about when you were a kid and you really wanted something. You would dream about having it and talk about having it constantly. You would do whatever you had to do in order to have the thing you wanted. Guess what would happen next? Nine out of ten times you would find a way to get it!

Many people lose that desire and creative thinking as they get older. We tend to accept only what we have or what we are given and do not try to get what we *really* want. We tell ourselves that it is "too hard or too expensive" or come up with a laundry list of excuses...*I'm too old, too young, I don't have enough education, I don't have enough money,* and anything else you can dream up. A child does not have any of those resources. All they think about is getting what they want! This is how *you* need to think. Don't get caught up in the details and all of the reasons why something can't or won't work. Think about what you want and set a goal and *go for it!* You just have to plant the seeds of desire and water them with belief and hard work. The universe will take care of the rest.

We thought about selling one hundred houses a year! It sounded crazy at the time. We had sold only a handful of houses, and here we were thinking about selling one hundred in a year! Fast-forward a few years and that is exactly what we did. One hundred houses in one year! It all starts with a thought. Everything you do every day starts with a thought, then your subconscious mind takes over and helps make your dreams a reality. Visualize exactly what you want and draw up an action plan to get it and have faith and believe that it will come to fruition. After you have the plan, you have to *take action*. This is why so many very intelligent people do not reach their goals. They know *what to do*, but they do not *take action*. You are taking action right now by reading this book. Chapter 1 will lay the foundation for developing the mindset of a million-dollar real estate investor.

ERIK AND MIKE'S BOTTOM LINE:
Set big goals, believe you can do it, and take action. That is the first step. The universe does the rest.

"Set a goal to become a millionaire but not for the money. Set a goal to become a millionaire for what it will make of you to achieve it."

—*Jim Rohn*

1

PSYCHOLOGY OF A MILLION-DOLLAR INVESTOR

Story from Mike: *It was a cool July morning in Lake Placid, New York. From a restaurant, I looked out the window at the mist rising up from the water on Mirror Lake. The sun was rising over the horizon, and the water temperature was a chilly sixty-one degrees. In just one short hour, I was going to dive in and start the 2.4-mile swim of my first-ever Ironman triathlon competition. My bike tires were pumped rock hard and my shoes were already clipped onto the pedals, ready to tackle the 112-mile hilly course. My running shoes were laid out with laces tied so I did not have to waste time getting started on the 26.2-mile marathon course.*

The horn blew for the 7:00 a.m. swim start and I thought I was in the perfect starting position. I tried to swim but kept getting clubbed in the back from other swimmers every time I tried to take a stroke. It felt like I was in a bar fight and was losing.

It turns out I was in one of the worst possible spots for starting the swim. I was right next to the first swim buoy that marked the start of the course and everyone seemed to be zeroing in on my swim spot so they could follow all of the course markers. I kicked and clubbed other swimmers to keep from drowning, and after about ten minutes, I finally found a little room to get into my rhythm. The race was under way. No turning back now.

My face was numb and my eyes bloodshot when I finally got out of the water. My goggles were hit and kicked by other swimmers several times and I swam most of the course with half-filled goggles. I slowly jogged to the transition area to start the bike ride. I stripped off my wetsuit, pulled on my shirt, and I was off. Getting out of the water onto the bike gave me a huge sense of relief. The swim is the only part of the race in which I really thought something could go wrong. As I settled into my bike rhythm, I started feeling an overwhelming sensation of excitement and joy. All of the training I had done to prepare for this race was behind me and the moment had finally arrived. I was racing in my first Ironman! I started talking to everyone and singing and yelling. I could not contain my emotions…I was higher than a kite. Endorphins are the best drug on the planet…thanks, Lord!

Reality set in at about mile forty. The course was hilly and I started to "feel" every mile. I settled down for the remaining seventy-two-mile bike course and started focusing on pedaling efficiently while I took in some much needed fuel. Several peanut butter and jelly sandwiches were crammed into my shirt pockets and I slowly washed them down with "Fierce Grape" Gatorade. Hot smashed sandwiches never tasted so good. The miles kept ticking away, and then, just past mile 111 of the bike course, I got a flat tire! LESS THAN ONE MILE TO GO before I could start the run! I could literally see the bike finish line down the road. I had two choices: change the tire or pick up the bike and run it over the finish line. I opted for the latter and I took off jogging with the bike over my shoulder.

I made it to the transition area, racked my bike, and slipped on my running shoes. The run started out great but turned ugly at about mile fourteen. My legs were toast. My spirit was willing but my body wasn't. Determined to finish the race, I had to do the old-man shuffle-walk-shuffle the remaining distance. I finally spotted the finish line and started to hear the cheers of the crowd. I was overwhelmed with emotion when I finally crossed the finish line. It took me ninety minutes longer than my time goal, but I finished. I didn't quit even though my body wanted to.

So what does an Ironman triathlon have to do with real estate investing and developing the psychology of a million-dollar investor?

> ***"Setting goals that stretch you are worth the pain! Even if you fall short of your goal, the fact that you set out to 'win the race' will get you much further than you may have ever imagined."***
>
> —*Mike Arch*

Before we get into the mechanics of creating and selling real estate notes, let's first talk about the mindset required to be successful in real estate.

PHILOSOPHY IS THE KEY TO SUCCESS

In this chapter, we are focusing on the biggest key to becoming a million-dollar real estate investor. That key is philosophy. That's right! Philosophy is the single most important factor in determining your success and reaching your big goals.

The reason philosophy is the most important is because it is the foundation on which all of your success is built. Jim Rohn used to refer to philosophy as the "set of the sail." The same wind blows on all of us, but those who know how to set the sail are the ones who win the race. To learn how to set your sail, it takes practice and repetition. If you want to get good at something, you need to work at it. If you don't have the right philosophy, when the sexy deal comes along or the million-dollar investor shows up, you won't have the tools in your mental toolbox to maximize those opportunities.

Take a look at this definition of *philosophy*: "The rational investigation of the truths and principles of being, knowledge, or conduct." In other words... searching for the truth and learning how to act on that truth. The great thing about the principles and philosophies taught in this book is that they are not new. There is no such thing as a "new" truth. Truth is truth, and discovering it is a fascinating process.

If you place an acorn in some soil and water it, it can grow into a giant oak tree that could live well over a hundred years. To grow the tree all we had to do was discover the truth that planting an acorn will grow into a huge tree! Nature does the rest! We don't need to understand *how* it works; we just need to discover this truth and act in accordance with nature.

Developing a million-dollar mindset is nothing more than discovering the success truths and planting those truths in your mind. Just like the acorn, planting the right philosophies and attitudes is all you have to do to get started on the road to becoming a millionaire. Nature will take over from there and the universe will provide the people and circumstances needed to help you become a million-dollar investor. It may sound a little strange, but just like a huge tree growing out of a tiny acorn, some things just can't be totally understood. There are many mysteries in this world and it's not important to know exactly WHY or HOW something works. It is just important to discover the truths and act in accordance with nature.

FIVE ROADBLOCKS TO AVOID

Before we get into some of the key principles for developing a million-dollar mindset, let's talk about some of the roadblocks you need to try to avoid:

ROADBLOCK ONE: YOU. You are potentially the number one roadblock to your own success. If you have not been very successful, you need to realize that your past does not equal your future. History is full of people who failed miserably in their past and then went on to great things. Take a deep breath and get out of your own way. Learn from your past, but don't let it keep you from moving forward. Today is the first day of the rest of your life. Replace any fear and doubt with faith. Remember, if other people have done it, you can too. You just have to believe that you can. Belief is the key and we will help you get there.

Take a look at the challenges and "failures" that Abraham Lincoln had to deal with prior to becoming the sixteenth president of the United States of America.

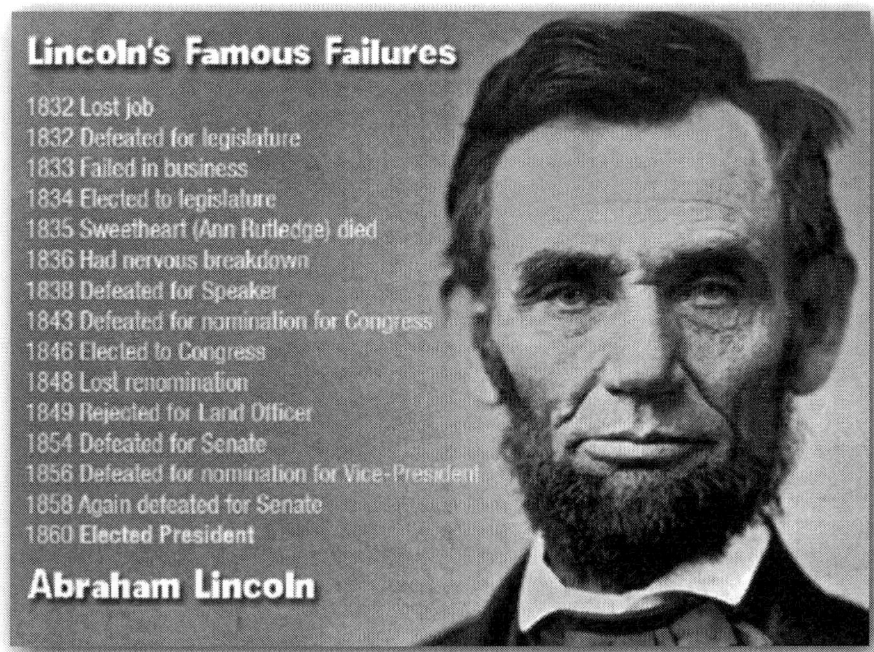

ROADBLOCK TWO: EXCUSES. Throw all of your excuses under the bus right now: *I'm too old, I'm too young, I don't have enough money, I don't have enough education,* etc. **FACT**: when you plant the right thoughts in your mind, nature takes over and the people and circumstances needed for your success somehow show up in your life. This truth in nature bears repeating: *when you plant the right thoughts in your mind, nature takes over and the people and circumstances needed for your success somehow show up in your life.* Just like the acorn growing into a huge tree…you don't need to understand *how* it works, you just need to discover the truth that it *works.*

ROADBLOCK THREE: NEGATIVE PEOPLE. Think about developing a million-dollar mindset as exercise for your brain. If you were training for an Ironman triathlon and all of the people you hung out with were fat and out of shape, you might want to start hanging around some people who are serious about their health and training. Negative people are the equivalent of fat and lazy training buddies. **FACT:** You can manage the amount of time you are spending with negative people. Limit your association with negative friends and family members and make a concerted effort to be around like-minded people. Some people may become jealous of your desire to become a million-dollar real estate investor and try to hold you down. You have to be cognizant of how much time you are spending with these people and be disciplined about limiting the time if necessary.

ROADBLOCK FOUR: NEGATIVE NEWS AND INFORMATION. You do not need to look very hard to find bad news. With the Internet and cable television, we are all bombarded with negative news twenty-four hours a day. Be diligent and guard your mind. We challenge you to take a thirty-day "news cleanse." Avoid watching any news on TV and don't read all of the "breaking news" on the Internet for thirty days. As you cleanse and purge your mind, you will be amazed how your outlook and attitude will change for the better.

Even if you think of yourself as a positive person, this cleanse will eliminate some of the garbage entering your mind and make room for high-octane positive thoughts. Don't underestimate the importance of this one. If you can make it for thirty days, we promise you will never go back. Don't worry: you won't miss anything major. Other people will keep you informed if the world is coming to an end. You are weeding the garden of your mind to prepare it for some new seeds.

ROADBLOCK FIVE: FEAR, INDECISION, AND DOUBT.

Story from Mike: *While I was considering signing up for my first Ironman triathlon, I was fearful that something might go wrong on the swim portion of the race. I was not a great swimmer and my mind imagined the worst scenarios you* *could dream up. I was very indecisive about making the commitment and I had a lot of doubt racing through my mind that I could successfully complete the event.*

Over the weeks and months prior to the race, I slowly built up my swimming distance and the fear started to be replaced with confidence. I entered several shorter races and my confidence and swimming ability grew. By the time it was Ironman race day, my mindset was bring it on! How did I go from being scared of drowning to bring it on? I took small action steps and built my confidence slowly but surely. Real estate investing and developing a million-dollar mindset works the same way. You start by educating yourself and then move toward doing your very first transaction. Slowly but surely you will become an Ironman real estate investor!

Irrational fear, doubt, and indecision are mind diseases. They need to be aggressively treated with positive thoughts and actions. If you are paralyzed by fear and thoughts are running through your mind like *I might fail, I might drown financially,* or *What will my friends think?* you need to defeat those thoughts by replacing fear with knowledge, action, and the right philosophies. Deep down your fears are begging to be squashed. Slowly squeeze them out by gaining knowledge, refining your philosophy, and taking action.

For people who have a fear of failure, for example, try this one on for size: How about choosing to adopt a philosophy and attitude that there is no such thing as failure? We believe that there are only *results*, and if we do not get the results we are after, we will learn from our results and do better next time. The truth about "failure" or any other event in life is this: the only meaning anything has is the meaning you give it. In other words, you can attach any meaning you want to events.

Early on in our flipping days, money was tight and we had multiple projects going on at one time. In one week we had several things stolen from three different properties. Two air-conditioning systems, one brand-new stove, and all of the electrical wiring was stripped from one of the houses. Our insurance policy had high deductibles and we did not want to file multiple claims, so we paid for everything out of our own pockets.

The following week we got a call from one of our contractors to inform us that someone had broken into one of our houses and started a huge fire in the living room. The house was a total loss. We both met at the house and then drove to the local coffee shop to discuss the situation. We could *choose* to believe that the real estate business is nothing but a bunch of headaches, we had invested in the wrong homes, and that everyone was out to get us. We could have decided it was time to get out of the business altogether and throw in the towel on real estate investing.

Instead, we chose to look at it this way: there are some people in life who are so lost and desperate they need to steal from others. Thank God they stole from us and burned our home and not a residence that was occupied where someone could have been seriously injured or killed. We talked about steps we were going to take to better secure our homes and install more exterior lighting. We also made a decision not to install appliances until the buyer is ready to move in. We learned from our past and kept moving forward. An investor with a million-dollar mindset is not going to let anything stand in his way on the path to millions. BS is just part of the game. We don't know anyone who has achieved any real measure of success who has not overcome significant obstacles on the way to the top. Failure is the stepping stone to success. Smile, pick yourself up and keep moving forward.

> ***"Every adversity you meet carries with it a seed of equivalent or greater benefit. Realize this statement, and believe in it. Close the door of your mind on all the failures and circumstances of your past so your mind can operate in a Positive Mental Attitude. Every problem has a solution... only you have to find it!***

> ***"If you will develop an 'I don't believe in defeat' attitude, you will learn that there is no such thing as defeat...until you accept it as such! If you can look at problems as temporary setbacks and stepping-stones to success, you will come to believe that the only limitations you have are the ones in your own mind.***
>
> ***"Remember, every defeat, every disappointment, and every adversity carries with it the seed of an equivalent or greater benefit."***
>
> —*Napoleon Hill*

In life and business you need to constantly refine your philosophy. One of the key philosophies we want to encourage you to embrace is the power and positive impact written goals have on your success.

GOAL SETTING

Remember what we talked about earlier about there being no "new" truths? Our mission is to help you discover the truths that will prepare you for becoming a million-dollar investor. One of the truths about setting goals is that you greatly increase the likelihood of reaching your goal if you write it down. Studies show that you are at least ten times more likely to reach a goal if it is in writing. You increase the odds of reaching the goal even more if you set a completion date and if you break the goal down into bite-size steps.

Just as you greatly increase the odds of the acorn growing into a tree if you give it plenty of water and sunshine; goals work the same way. Work with the universe...write down your goals with a date for their completion and break them into small steps. Whenever you set a goal, take at least one action step toward the goal immediately. Even if the step seems almost insignificant. Order a book, look up a phone number, or send an e-mail to schedule a meeting.

Momentum is a real force in nature and it is up to you to get the ball rolling. Give the ball one little push immediately after you set a goal. Getting the ball rolling in the right direction is key. Don't worry about the destination…direction is the key. You will arrive in due time.

Another truth about goals is that you have the choice to set huge goals or tiny goals. Just as in nature, you can plant an acorn and grow a huge oak or you can plant a mustard seed and grow a mustard plant. The choice is yours. Nature does not care which seeds you plant. The soil, rain, and sunshine have the same effect on all seeds. Take a look at this poem found in Napoleon Hill's classic success book *Think and Grow Rich* to help illustrate this point.

I bargained with life for a penny
and life would pay no more,
however, I begged at evening
when I counted my scanty store;
For life is a just employer
he gives you what you ask
but, once you have set the wages
why, you must bear the task;
I worked for a menial's hire
only to learn dismayed
that any wage I had asked of life,
life would have willingly paid.

— Jessie B. Rittenhouse

When we talk about goal setting, we have to refine our philosophy on the subject. Many people associate big goals with a lot of hard work. Those people are probably correct. Big goals take a while to accomplish and often require a lot of hard work. Why not set some small goals and just "get by" in life, someone may ask. The million-dollar investor knows that by setting large goals, he is going to have to stretch himself to reach them and will grow significantly in the process. Don't settle for average! Ask anyone who has climbed the mountain of success and she will tell you…it was worth it! Set huge goals and become more.

MONEY

The million-dollar investor knows that money is not evil and can be used to do some amazing positive things. We would agree that there are some evil ways of obtaining money, but money, in and of itself, is not evil. This may be obvious to you, but you would be surprised how much mental baggage people are carrying around with them about what having money means. Million-dollar investors have learned the truth that there is an abundance of money in circulation and that the way to get more is to be a good steward of the money they currently have. When you take care of the money you have and invest it responsibly and wisely, the universe entrusts you with more.

Take a look at the following parable from an ancient Bible text to illustrate this truth:

THE PARABLE OF THE BAGS OF GOLD

> *Again, it will be like a man going on a journey who called his servants and entrusted his wealth to them. To one he gave five bags of gold, to another two bags, and to another one bag, each according to his ability. Then he went on his journey. The man who had received five bags of gold went at once and put his money to work and gained five bags more. So also, the one with two bags of gold gained two more. But the man who had received one bag went off, dug a hole in the ground and hid his master's money.*
>
> *After a long time the master of those servants returned and settled accounts with them. The man who had received five bags of gold brought the other*

five. "Master," he said, "you entrusted me with five bags of gold. See, I have gained five more."

His master replied, "Well done, good and faithful servant! You have been faithful with a few things; I will put you in charge of many things. Come and share your master's happiness!"

The man with two bags of gold also came. "Master," he said, "you entrusted me with two bags of gold; see…I have gained two more."

His master replied, "Well done, good and faithful servant! You have been faithful with a few things; I will put you in charge of many things. Come and share your master's happiness!"

Then the man who had received one bag of gold came. "Master," he said, "I knew that you are a hard man, harvesting where you have not sown and gathering where you have not scattered seed. So I was afraid and went out and hid your gold in the ground. See, here is what belongs to you."

His master replied, "you wicked, lazy servant! So you knew that I harvest where I have not sown and gather where I have not scattered seed? Well then, you should have put my money on deposit with the bankers, so that when I returned I would have received it back with interest.

So take the bag of gold from him and give it to the one who has ten bags. For whoever has, will be given more and they will have an abundance. Whoever does not have, even what they have will be taken from them. And throw that worthless servant outside, into the darkness, where there will be weeping and gnashing of teeth.

Whether you have a thousand dollars to invest or a million, invest it wisely and more will be entrusted to you. That is the way the universe works. It would be the *wrong* philosophy to believe that *when I have a lot of money, I will invest it wisely, but since I don't have much money, it really doesn't matter. Wrong*! Being a good steward over *whatever* has been entrusted to you is the key to receiving more.

COMPOUNDING WEALTH

Story from Mike: *Whenever my family gets together for a holiday or other special occasions and a meal is served, everyone asks my mother if she can bring the dessert. The reason everyone wants Mom to bring the dessert is because her pies are world-class. She has been making pies for about fifty years now. There is something about her pies that nobody can resist. The crust is golden brown and flaky and there is always the perfect ratio of crust to fruit filling. The pies are cooked to perfection and they always taste delicious, not too sweet and not too tart. She is an expert at apple, cherry, and blueberry and nails it every time.*

When people ask my mom how she does it, she just says that she has done it hundreds of times and knows all of the little tricks to make the pies turn out perfectly. From the way she rolls out the pie crust, the way she prepares the fruit filling, to the oven temperature and baking time, she has the recipe dialed in. My mom is a really good cook as well, but her pies are over the top.

When we started out in the real estate investment game, we were trying to flip homes from $20,000 to $300,000 and everything in between. When we were trying to reach our goal of creating passive income, we tried renting single-family homes, multifamily properties, and even mobile homes. Since we were trying to cook up so many different real estate recipes, we never got really good at one dish. Then we found the recipe for seller-financing. When we focused all of our energy on perfecting our seller-financing recipe, we started making consistent profits and still provided our note buyers with solid double-digit returns. We now produce a perfect golden brown real estate note with flaky crust every time!

We want to illustrate the value of a "great" recipe compared to a "good" recipe by showing you some compounded returns over time. Acquiring rental properties has been the investment vehicle of choice for many real estate investors trying to build passive income. We agree that rentals can be a pretty "good" recipe but definitely not as good as building a portfolio of real estate notes. Not only are the yields better, but with real estate notes you don't have to deal with renters, repairs, property taxes, insurance, and vacancy rates.

Most experienced investors that focus on renting properties would consider an 8 percent net return very good performance of their portfolio. Our typical real estate notes sold to private investors yield about a 12 percent net return. If you learn the steps taught in this book to actually create your own notes, you could yield about 16 percent! These are the same dollars, just a different recipe.

One of the biggest reasons many investors choose to go the rental-home route is because they can use leverage by getting a loan from a bank to enhance their returns. Guess what? You can leverage notes too and we will show you how in the following chapters.

Don't underestimate the power of earning a higher return over time. Take a look at the following numbers to see how earning a higher yield is the difference between an average retirement and an extraordinary one. The following example assumes you are reinvesting your annual return each year.

$100,000 invested at 8 percent for thirty years grows to: $1,006,265.69
$100,000 invested at 12 percent for thirty years grows to: $2,995,992.95
$100,000 invested at 16 percent for thirty years grows to: $8,584,987.69

Which path would you rather take? The average path of 8 percent or the extraordinary one at 16 percent? The time is going to go by either way. Don't settle for average in anything in your life!

> ***"The orderliness of the world of natural laws gives evidence that they are under the control of a universal plan.***
>
> ***"Man is the only living creature equipped with the power of choice through which he may establish his own thought and behavior patterns. You have the power to break bad habits and to create good ones in their place...at will.***
>
> ***"You are where you are and what you are because of your established habits and thoughts and deeds."***
>
> —*Napoleon Hill*

Let's finish this chapter by continuing to build the foundation of a million-dollar investor. Adopting the ten core principles of a million-dollar investor will help prepare you for launching your real estate investment career in a big way.

TEN CORE PRINCIPLES OF THE MILLION-DOLLAR INVESTOR:

1. TAKING FULL RESPONSIBILTY FOR EVERYTHING IN YOUR LIFE

Million-dollar investors take 100 percent responsibility for what happens in their lives. They don't blame the government, global warming, or other people for anything that happens to them. Not enough money in their savings account? Their spending choices are the cause. Fifty pounds over their ideal weight? They don't blame McDonald's, Burger King, and Coca-Cola. They point to the man in the mirror. Tired and cranky due to not enough sleep? They don't blame *Monday Night Football* or Jimmy Fallon. Didn't get the job promotion? They ask themselves, *What can I start doing now to prepare myself for the next opportunity?*

Even though it is very tempting to want to blame someone else for your life circumstances, million-dollar investors have learned the truth about taking full responsibility for everything in their lives: this is one of the most powerful practices you can adopt! When you can only blame yourself for things, you know whom to work on. If you had to fix the government and everyone else, there would be absolutely no chance of making your life better. Focus on becoming a better version of YOU by consistently educating yourself and refining your philosophy. It wouldn't hurt to ask for a little help and guidance from the Big Guy upstairs, too.

One of the most debilitating things many people deal with is their childhood upbringing. It is sad that many people were dealt a bad hand as a child. As sad and rough as some people had it, use it as fuel to forge a much better future. The past does not equal your future.

Another truth in the same vain as personal responsibility is the subject of discipline. Million-dollar investors have learned the truth that you can't fake success and that you can't live a balanced, productive life if you don't exercise discipline in *all* areas of your life. If you don't take care of your health, your performance at work will suffer. If you don't build and maintain loving relationships with your family, your work won't be as rewarding. If you lie and cheat on your taxes, there is a good chance you will lie and cheat in other areas of your life. Jim Rohn teaches "All disciplines affect one another." Million-dollar investors live with integrity and strive for excellence in all areas of their lives.

2. DAILY ACTION STEPS

Million-dollar investors understand that knowledge is *not* power. Knowledge put into *action* is power. They also understand the truth that momentum is real and even the smallest nudge can get things moving in the right direction.

Million-dollar investors write down their goals and take daily action toward them, no matter how small and insignificant the action may be. The compounding effect of daily actions consistently moves them toward their goals and pays huge dividends over time.

3. THE VALUE OF TIME

Eighty percent of the money is made by 20 percent of the people in the world. The 20 percent have figured out how to use their time wisely and focus on things that will be high payoff activities. Million-dollar investors understand the truth that time is more valuable than money *and* is their most valuable resource. They focus on creating passive income and investing their time in being productive in both their business and personal lives. Television watching is usually at the bottom of the priority list for million-dollar investors.

4. THE POWER OF CHOOSING WHAT TO BELIEVE

There was a man who was terrified by the thought of speaking in public. Throughout his life, he avoided any situation in which he would have to get up in front of a group of people. He was convinced that there was no way he could ever do anything resembling public speaking. When his father died, his mother asked him if he would say a few words at the funeral. The man had been very close to his father and couldn't say no to his mother. He was an only child and felt he had to do it. He wrote out a few paragraphs in preparation for the funeral and practiced every day for his first-ever public speaking experience. The day of the funeral, he was so nervous he almost passed out thinking about having to get up in front of the crowd. His father was a well-known businessman in town, and his family expected quite a crowd.

The time finally came in the service when it was his turn to speak. He walked up to the microphone with his notes in hand and started to read what he had written. He told stories of when his dad used to take him fishing and several other special moments with his father. He even told a few funny stories and got a few laughs from the crowd. After the funeral service, several people came up to him and told him how much they enjoyed his eulogy and what a good job he had done. The same positive message was affirmed to him over and over again. Even the priest came up to him afterward and told him what a great job he had done. Before this day, he would have never believed in a million years that he could do any public speaking. As he laid his head down on his pillow that night, he smiled and decided he actually enjoyed speaking, and the positive feedback was something he rarely experienced. Over the next few months he started looking for more opportunities to get up in front of people. He ended up joining a public speaking group and became a really good public speaker!

Million-dollar investors understand the process and power of belief. How can you become a million-dollar investor if you have never done one real estate transaction in your life? The answer is to convince yourself you *can* by telling yourself you *can* and then acting "as if" you already *have* become one. Think of this process as planting seeds in a garden. If you plant lots of seeds, water them, and weed the garden, chances are those seeds will germinate and grow. If you plant seeds of belief in your mind by telling yourself you are a million-dollar investor, for example, and start acting as though you are, you will slowly start to see yourself in that way. It's almost like you have to convince your brain by affirming what you want. If you tell yourself something over and over you will eventually start seeing evidence of your desired belief. The more you affirm your belief and take action "as if" you already have the belief, it will start to materialize.

It's not that you tricked your brain into believing something that is false. Your brain never had any evidence that you were a million-dollar investor, so it did not believe it. When you start affirming a belief, it's like the brain says, "OK…I now have evidence and will start moving toward making that belief true." What actually happened is you helped that seed grow by acting as though you already were a million-dollar investor, and slowly but surely, evidence for the belief starts to appear. Anyone who has been successful at anything in life had to first *believe*. When you affirm something over and over again, you bridge the gap between nonbelief and belief.

Affirmation is the equivalent of water and sunshine to the planted acorn. Exactly how it works is a mystery. All we know is that the brain works that way. Go with it...write down "I am a million-dollar investor and am in the process of becoming an expert at real estate investing." Write it down and put it in three places: on your mirror in the bathroom where you brush your teeth, on the nightstand next to the bed, and on the dashboard of your car. Make a commitment to read it out loud five times a day for thirty days, and watch what happens. You WILL believe it and be well on your way to becoming a million-dollar real estate investor.

5. MASTER ONE RECIPE AND BECOME AN EXPERT

The million-dollar investor has learned that you don't make any real progress in life being a jack-of-all-trades. Being an expert at something and mastering the recipe is where the money is. When we were flipping houses in all price ranges, buying mobile homes, renting houses, and also trying to do traditional real estate brokerage, we were working our tails off and just barely getting by. We were jacks-of-all-trades. When we decided to focus on producing real estate notes within a specific price range, our business exploded.

6. THE POWER OF FOCUSED CONCENTRATION

Million-dollar investors have discovered the truth about focused concentration. Just like holding a magnifying glass in the sun to burn a blade of grass, the same principle applies to focused thought. When you need to solve an important problem or are trying to deal with an important issue, picture your mind like the magnifying glass. Close the door, silence the phone, turn off the TV, and forget multitasking! This is a skill that must be mastered if you are serious about building wealth. Think of focus as a muscle. Just like when you go to the gym to lift weights, practice focusing on the important people and issues in your life. Don't let distractions get the best of you and steal your wealth. Practice the art of focused concentration. It pays big money.

7. THE POWER OF A REAL DECISION

Million-dollar investors understand the importance of making real decisions. The word *decision* literally means "to cut off from." In other words, when you make a decision, you are cutting off your other options.

There was a military commander in ancient times who decided to attack an island. He knew the island would be the ideal location for a strategic port, and he had to have it. He had three ships full of soldiers sneak onto the southern shore in the middle of the night and then he ordered his men to burn the ships. The commander wanted to have no other option except to win or die. Retreat was not an option. The battle ensued and they won decisively. Practice the art of making real decisions. Make thoughtful decisions and be slow to change once you make one.

8. THE POWER OF A TEAM

Million-dollar investors understand the power of building a team of like-minded, focused people. Once again, this is a truth that has been revealed in nature. When multiple like-minded people work together, the group dynamic produces results that no individual could create. It could be likened to logs being thrown on a fire together. When the logs are close to one another, they burn extremely hot and produce a beautiful fire. If you take the logs and lay them individually on the ground, they slowly fizzle out. Find someone who wants to go on the wealth journey with you and enjoy the ride. You will get there much faster with someone by your side.

> ***"The Mastermind principle consists of an alliance of two or more minds working in perfect harmony for the attainment of a common definite objective.***

"No two minds ever come together without a third invisible force, which may be likened to a 'third mind.' When a group of individual minds are coordinated and function in harmony, the increased energy created through that alliance becomes available to every individual in the group.

"No man can become a permanent success without taking others along with him."

—*Napoleon Hill*

9. GETTING RICH SLOWLY IS THE WAY OF THE WEALTHY

Million-dollar investors have the ability to think long term. They are focused on the direction they are going in but are not overly concerned about when they arrive at their destination. They understand that building significant lasting wealth takes time. They view themselves first as investors and are always cognizant of how they spend their money. Million-dollar investors are not impulse buyers. They are focused on creating passive income and have mastered the art of enjoying the ride while in pursuit of their financial independence.

10. GIVING BACK

Jim Rohn taught us that "giving starts the receiving process," even though intuition tells you that by giving you will have *less*. The truth that has been discovered by million-dollar investors is that giving with a pure heart actually brings more abundance into their lives. There is a higher power at work here, and the mind of man cannot totally comprehend why nature works this way. When you give of your resources, it demonstrates to the universe that you believe in abundance and you are being a good steward of the resources you have been entrusted with. It really is true that giving is better than receiving. Ancient Bible scripture has numerous verses illustrating this truth:

> "Give and it will be given to you. Good measure, pressed down, shaken together, running over, will be put into your lap. For with the measure you use it will be measured back to you."

> "One gives freely, yet grows all the richer; another withholds what he should give, and only suffers want. Whoever brings blessing will be enriched, and one who waters will himself be watered."

> "Each one must give as he has decided in his heart, not reluctantly or under compulsion, for God loves a cheerful giver."

Now that we understand the foundational thinking of a million-dollar investor, let's continue our journey on the path to wealth and talk about some of the common investment strategies in the next chapter.

ERIK AND MIKE'S BOTTOM LINE:
Get the negative news and negative people out of your life and stop making excuses. If you want to build lasting wealth, invest time on a weekly basis on personal development so you can refine your philosophy. Just like working out at a gym, the more you practice, the better you will get.

"Accurate thought involves two fundamentals. First, you must separate facts from mere information. Second, you must separate facts into two classes—the important and the unimportant. Only by doing so can you think clearly and accurately. Accurate thinkers permit no one to do their thinking for them. Gather information and listen to the opinions of others, but reserve for yourself the privilege of making decisions."

—*Napoleon Hill*

2

COMMON INVESTMENT STRATEGIES

There are many different strategies for making money in real estate. This book focuses on seller financing and creating and selling real estate notes. Throughout this book, the term "seller financing" and "owner financing" are used interchangeably. In this chapter, we are going to touch on three alternative strategies and compare them to the seller financing business model. We spend a little more time on the contract assignment strategy because if you are just starting out in the business, contract assignments are a great way to generate cash and learn the business with minimal risk. The three alternative strategies are:

1. Contract assignments
2. Rental properties
3. Flipping houses

CONTRACT ASSIGNMENTS

Let's start with contract assignments, which is also known as "wholesaling." The idea behind contract assignments, or wholesaling, is to find a motivated seller who is willing to sell you their property at a price below market value. The contract you sign with the seller gives you the right to buy the house, and includes an option period for *you* to opt out of the contract. Many "wholesalers" give the seller only $50 for the right to opt out of the contract. This is the option fee. This is a legal and ethical way of doing business as long as you are totally up-front with the seller. The idea is to find a house below market price, then “assign the contract” within your “option period” for a *higher* price. The bottom line with this strategy, is that you *never have to take any money out of your pocket except the $50* option fee! Below, we have outlined a case study to help you understand how a typical wholesale transaction might work.

We received a phone call from a homeowner who saw an ad we were running in the local newspaper. The ad read, “I BUY HOUSES.” The homeowner called, and this was how the dialogue went:

Homeowner: Hello, I saw your ad in the newspaper that said you buy homes. I have a home that I want to sell.

Erik: Great…thanks for calling me. What’s your name?

Homeowner: Suzy.

Erik: Hi, Suzy, can you tell me a little about the house and give me the address?

Homeowner: It has three bedrooms and one bath. It was built in the 1940s, and it is located at 322 Fair Avenue.

Erik: Thanks, Suzy. How long have you been trying to sell your home?

Homeowner: I just started calling people today. I inherited the house from my father. It used to be a rental home that he had for many years.

Erik: Great. How much are you trying to sell it for?

Homeowner: I’m not sure. I just want to get the best price that I can.

Erik: Suzy, do you own the house free and clear, or is there a loan at the bank that needs to be paid off?

Homeowner: I own it free and clear.

Erik: Great! Does the home need any repairs?

Homeowner: Yes, the tenants that just moved out trashed the place, and I don't want to deal with it anymore.

Erik: No problem, Suzy. We can buy your house as is.

Homeowner: Perfect!

Erik: What do you think your house is worth?

Homeowner: My neighbor across the street sold his home a couple of months ago for $85,000.

Erik: How was the condition of that home compared to yours?

Homeowner: I think it was recently remodeled and in pretty good condition.

Erik: OK…Suzy. I am interested in your house and would like to make you a cash offer today. What time could I meet you at the house to take a look?

Homeowner: How about three o'clock today?

Erik: Perfect, Suzy. I'll see you later today at three o'clock.

The goal of the initial phone call is to ask a few questions to see if you might be able to make a deal and avoid wasting your time. Assuming this is the case, you will then want to schedule a time to see the house ASAP. Oftentimes, homeowners will call several investors on the same day. We want to stress how important it is to look at the house as quickly as possible. Typically, the first investor to see the property gets it under contract. There have been several times we have been on our way to an appointment when we received a phone call from the seller informing us that they just signed a contract with another investor. That sucks!

Please note that we used the homeowners name several times during the conversation. One's own name is one of the sweetest sounds in the English language. It makes people feel more comfortable when you use their name during the conversation. Real estate investing requires interaction with people and if you expect to be successful, be nice and pay attention to things that you might have in common so you can build rapport.

Story from Mike: *A couple of years ago, I was negotiating directly with a seller on a property that I really wanted. Deborah was a single woman in her sixties and a tough negotiator. She was selling her mother's home and was standing firm on her asking price. She had called me because of an ad and when I first arrived at the house I was greeted with a firm handshake and something close to a scowl on her face. Arms crossed, she gave me a one-minute tour of the three-bedroom, two-bath house and proceeded to tell me "the price is $110,000 and it is not negotiable." I felt like I just got kicked in the groin, and her steely eyes could have burned a hole right through me.*

I knew the market well and loved the area. If I could purchase the home for $95,000, I could make a decent profit. I tried to make some small talk before I was going to hit her up with my offer. I asked if I could take a walk around the outside of the house, and she agreed. While walking around, I mentioned that I had two children and asked her if she had any. She said "No, and I never wanted any." (Strike one)! Then I said, "What a beautiful day! Isn't this weather fantastic?" She *quickly responded, "It is supposed to get up to ninety-five degrees out today and it is going to be miserable. I am from up north and hate the damn Texas weather." (Strike two)! Finally I said, "I'm from up north too." She asked where from, and I said "In Wisconsin…Green Bay Packer country" (the Packers had just won the Super Bowl that year).*

Deborah immediately changed her demeanor and started being really talkative and friendly. It turns out that she had also grown up in Wisconsin and was a HUGE Packers fan. We went inside and reminisced about the big game and she even went back to her closet and brought out her collection of Packers jerseys and her "cheese head." She offered me a soda and we sat and talked about the Packers and Wisconsin for about twenty minutes.

Finally the conversation circled back to the house. I explained to her that my goal with the house was to fix it up and bring it back to its glory days and sell it to a new family. She appreciated the fact that I was not going to turn it into a rental property. I explained to her that I was not trying to get rich off of her house but that I did need to buy it at a price at which I could make a reasonable profit. I told her the most I could pay was $95,000. She paused and thought about it for just a moment and said, "You got a deal." We shook hands and I broke out the contract to get it in writing.

Not all negotiations have a happy ending, but if you can find something you have in common with the person you are negotiating with, chances are things will go better. The definition of *rapport* is "when two or more people feel that they are in sync or on the same wavelength because they feel similarly or relate well to each other." The goal is to find something in common so you can relate to each other.

Some of our favorite topics of conversation for building rapport are sports teams, children, and current events. Guess what people like to talk about? *Themselves*! If you walk into a house and see a picture of the guy you are meeting holding a big fish on a boat, ask him about the experience, and start talking about fishing. If you see pictures of kids everywhere, start asking about their kids. This is not manipulation. This is just a great way to get to know the person you are dealing with and to make them feel comfortable. People like to buy and sell from people they like and trust. Building rapport helps to facilitate that process.

Now, back to our case study. Keep in mind that the following dialogue is the way we would handle a wholesale deal. Our goal is to get the house under contract, find a buyer, and then assign the contract to them *without actually spending our own money to purchase the house.* When we arrive at the house, the conversation would go something like this:

Erik: Hi Suzy, I'm Erik Saengerhausen. Thanks for meeting with me today. I really appreciate the call. Let's take a good look at the house and then talk numbers.

Suzy: OK…

Erik: Thanks for showing me the house. It obviously needs quite a bit of work. How old is the roof?

Suzy: I'm not sure.

Erik: Are there any plumbing or electrical problems that you are aware of?

Suzy: The light in the hall quit working a while back, and the tub drains a little slowly.

Erik: How are your neighbors?

Suzy: The ones to the left are an older retired couple. The ones to the right just remodeled their house and have two children.

Erik: What do you think your house is worth?

Suzy: Probably about $65,000.

Erik: How did you come up with that number?

Suzy: I know it needs a lot of work, and my neighbors sold for $85,000.

Erik: Your neighbor's house at $85,000 was updated and move-in ready. Your house needs a lot of rehab, and from an investor's perspective, it is only worth $50,000. If you agree to the price, I will even pay all the closing costs and haul off the trash.

Let's say you haggle a bit and get the seller to agree to $53,000. Now that you have a verbal agreement, it is critical that you get the seller to sign a contract. Always have a contract with you and get the agreement in writing ASAP.

Now that we have agreed on a firm sales price, we would say the following if we were going to wholesale the house:

"Suzy, let's go over the paperwork. What this contract basically says is that you are agreeing to sell us your home for $53,000, and that we plan on closing within thirty days. There is an option period for us to opt out of the contract within fourteen days if we choose to do so. We want to get our contractors over here to inspect the property. Ninety-five percent of the time, we are on the same page, but we always like another set of eyes on all of the homes that we buy. By the way, we are paying you $50 for the fourteen-day option period. If we decide not to buy the house and cancel the contract, you get to keep the $50. Of course, we do not anticipate having to opt out of the contract. You will also notice on the contract that the buyer is listed as "The Note Factory and/or Assigns." We often assign contracts to fellow investors. Since the house is vacant, would you mind if we put a lockbox on the property with your key in it so we do not have to bother you every time we look at the property? We want to start getting bids from contractors right away, and start showing it to a couple of other investors."

We really like to get our hands on a key and push hard to get one. We tell the seller that we don't want to bother them every time we take someone by the house. If the home is occupied, it is much more challenging to coordinate with a homeowner (or worse, a tenant) every time you show the house. Wholesaling VACANT homes is much easier than wholesaling occupied homes. With regard to the closing date, option period, and option fee, all of these items are negotiable.

Now that you have a contract, you have fourteen days to assign the contract to another investor or opt out. You have a lot to potentially gain and a whopping $50 to lose if you have to opt out of the contract. Talk about a low-risk real estate deal!

> ***"Let others lead small lives, but not you...Let others argue over small things, but not you...Let others cry over small hurts, but not you...Let others leave their future in someone else's hands, but not you."***
>
> ***—Jim Rohn***

Remember, in this case study, we are talking about a WHOLESALE property. The goal is to get the property under contact, find a buyer, and assign the contract during your option period. By the way, we love wholesalers! Wholesalers call us consistently, and say, "I've got a great deal for you. I have a property under contract for $62,000, and I will assign the contract to you for a $5,000 fee. If you agree to pay $67,000 it's yours."

Deals like these represent some of the most profitable real estate transactions we do each year, even after paying the "contract assignment fee." These fees vary greatly. The typical range is $3,000 to $10,000, but they can be much higher depending upon the price point and potential profit on the deal. We primarily deal in homes that retail for under $100,000. If you find a good deal, it will not be hard to assign the contract quickly to an investor. Investors are constantly looking for good deals. Just don't get too greedy and ask for an unreasonable fee. A quick $5,000 when you are just starting out is a nice little payday.

HOW DO YOU FIND WHOLESALE DEALS?

1. Run **I BUY HOUSES** ads in local newspapers.
2. Put up **I BUY HOUSES** signs in the neighborhoods investors like to buy in.
3. Find a good Realtor and ask them to e-mail you *all* of their new listings within your targeted price point and area. If you find a deal, try to get it under contract quickly. (Most Realtors can program the Multiple Listing Service to e-mail you new listings automatically. Your Realtor sets you up in the system and then it's on autopilot.)
4. Drive through neighborhoods and look for vacant or abandoned homes. Look up the address on the county property tax website, and mail the homeowner a letter asking them if they would like to sell their home. Also, be sure to talk to the neighbors. Ask them if they know the story on the house and if they have any contact information for the homeowner.

Once you find a house, you'll need to find someone to "assign" or "wholesale" it to. Building a list of investors or potential buyers is relatively easy.

HOW DO YOU BUILD YOUR INVESTOR LIST?

1. Contact everyone who runs WE BUY HOUSES ads in newspapers.
2. Contact HomeVestors franchise owners (the "WE BUY UGLY HOUSES" people).
3. Google "CASH HOME BUYERS" and call everyone who comes up on your search.
4. Many cities have a real estate investors association. Go to the meetings, and get as many phone numbers and e-mail addresses as you can. Network, network, network.

This was just a brief overview of the concept of contract assignments. Once again, this book is focused on the power of creating passive income with the seller-finance business model. The goal in this chapter is to expose you to other common real estate investment strategies so you can compare them with our preferred model.

RENTAL PROPERTIES

Renting properties has been the investment vehicle of choice for some investors and has worked well for many. Our personal experience dealing with rentals has been mediocre at best. We are not after average results or average yields. Average is easy. We are after extraordinary results, and seller financing has given us those results. Here are some questions to help you better understand the difference between seller financing and being a landlord:

- *Would you rather collect a payment from a tenant with a renter's mentality or from a homeowner who has pride of ownership?*
- *Would you sleep better at night knowing that you collected a small rent deposit from a tenant or $15,000 down from a homeowner?*
- *Would you rather sell your home to one person who stays there for twenty years and pays you like an ATM or rent to twenty different families over the same period of time and deal with a steady dose of repair issues and vacancies between renters?*

- *Would you rather pay the property taxes and homeowner association dues or have the person living in the house pay them?*
- *Would you rather earn an 8 percent yield on your money or a 16 percent yield? This book will show you how to get 16 percent or higher with our seller-finance strategy!*

Being a landlord and acquiring rental properties is an option for real estate investors, but our experience has shown us there is a better way: seller financing!

FLIPPING PROPERTIES

This is the strategy many people refer to when they think about making money in real estate: buy a house cheap, fix it up, and flip it for a profit.

There are many good courses and books on how to become a successful "house flipper." We have flipped literally hundreds of homes and it is our least favorite strategy. Here's why:

1. **INSPECTORS:** When you do a flip, most buyers will be working with a Realtor, and 99 percent of Realtors recommend hiring a professional home inspector. Inspectors perform a valuable service, but they also scare off a good percentage of buyers. We have seen inspection reports on homes that have been meticulously maintained that still have significant inspection issues. Inspectors WILL find issues with the home, and the buyer's Realtor will probably ask you to deal with some or ALL of the repairs. These repairs will significantly eat into your profits. (When you offer seller financing, you are bringing so much value to the buyer you can sell your homes AS IS. The buyer is welcome to get an inspection and we encourage them to do so. However, since you are offering financing, YOU are in control. You can choose to do the repairs or choose not to do the repairs, and chances are it will not affect the buyer's decision to move forward with the purchase.)

2. **PRIOR MLS LISTING HISTORY:** Oftentimes, the properties we buy to flip are found in the Multiple Listing Service. After we do a total rehab and relist it in the MLS for sale, every Realtor knows exactly what we paid for the home and what we are trying to sell it for. Realtors often use these facts to try to negotiate a much lower price since they know the home is being "flipped." (In a typical owner-finance deal, we do not list our homes in the MLS, and this becomes a nonissue.) Later in this book we will show you how to market and sell your properties in less than thirty days without listing it with a Realtor.
3. **REALTORS:** Being licensed real estate professionals, we have a lot of respect for Realtors, who make their living by commission only. Realtors provide a valuable service, but, of course, they also expect to get paid a commission. The SELLER typically pays the commission. (In a typical seller-finance deal using our system, no other Realtors are involved since the homes are not listed in the MLS system. A buyer is welcome to have a Realtor represent them, but the BUYER must pay their commission.)
4. **APPRAISERS:** Most traditional mortgage companies require an appraisal of the home you are selling. There is nothing more frustrating than a buyer who falls in love with one of our homes only to have the appraiser come along and say the house is only worth $170,000 instead of $175,000. We have a question for you to ponder. If appraisers can only use previous sales to justify values, how can values ever go up? We have asked this question many times and have never gotten a straight answer from anyone. If you have a willing buyer and a willing seller agreeing on price and terms, then in our book, the home appraises. (In a typical owner-finance transaction, no appraisal is required. We always try to price our homes at market value, so if the homeowner wants to refinance down the road, he will be able to. Also, we would strongly argue the point that since owner financing is being offered on a property, **the appraised value on the home should be**

higher due to the terms offered. Most appraisals DO NOT include any added value for the terms of financing being offered to the home buyer.)

5. **MORTGAGE COMPANIES/BANKS:** Many mortgage companies and banks have "FLIP" rules to help "protect the consumer." I guess somewhere along the way, there were some dishonest appraisers, loan officers, investors, and Realtors, and "flipped" properties got a bad reputation. This is really frustrating when you are truly trying to bring value to the real estate marketplace by purchasing a distressed property, investing your hard-earned money into the home, and trying to sell it at a reasonable market value. Isn't this the American dream? Invest your money into something, make it better than you found it, and sell it for a profit? For reasons we will never fully understand, the government, mortgage companies, and banks all seem to have a problem with flipped properties. Sometimes, lenders won't lend money on a home that was sold within the past three to twelve months, and will often request two separate appraisal reports. I guess this is to make sure one of the appraisers is not in cahoots with the seller or Realtor and inflating its appraised value. By the way, in the case of FHA loans, the lender requests two appraisals and only allows the buyer to pay for one. Guess who has to pay for the other one? *You*! Also, lenders frequently ask us to e-mail them a list of all the repairs we have done on the house—*and* proof of what we paid for the home. They want this information *even after it has appraised* at full value! *twice*! We usually tell them to take a hike and that we paid $1 for the house. The house either appraises or it doesn't! What business is it of theirs what we paid for the house? As you can see, this is a touchy subject with us. (With a typical seller-financed property, there are no "FLIP" rules that get in the way of a smooth transaction.)

You can make some money flipping houses, but a combination of all the issues finally drove us to find a better way. Guess what? We found it!

ERIK AND MIKE'S BOTTOM LINE:
Wholesaling is a great way to get into the game if you don't have a lot of money. Flipping properties is hard, and dealing with tenants is a headache. This is why most people that get into the real estate business don't last. They have the wrong recipe.

"Days are expensive. When you spend a day you have one less day to spend. So make sure you spend each one wisely."

—Jim Rohn

3

WHY SELLER FINANCING? PASSIVE INCOME ROCKS!

Most people somewhere along the way came across a get-rich-quick scheme, only to have their dreams shattered and their money lost when they realized it was a scam. Get-rich-quick schemes and lottery tickets are for suckers. True wealth and success comes from patience, perseverance, and focus on becoming an expert at something. Our goal with this book is to put you on the path to becoming an expert at owner financing and help you build wealth and passive income that will last for generations. The big house on the hill and the one-thousand-acre ranch are all within reach if you are willing to get rich the right way: slowly and steadily.

Our owner-finance strategies will teach you how to earn large amounts of money, *and* that money will flow into your bank account *passively* every month! Passive income is ultimately what provides you the privilege of living like the wealthy. Passive income allows you to travel the world in style on your schedule, not your boss's schedule. Why not take a two-month vacation instead of a two-week vacation? Why not be in a position to donate 50 percent of your income instead of 10 percent? Why not buy a house on the beach *and* in the mountains?

We are not saying that money is the only thing that makes someone rich. Some of the richest people we know earn very modest incomes. Many people are rich in relationships and health, and we are all rich because we are children of God. Money is just one type of wealth, but why not go for it? It is within your reach if you study and practice the strategies and philosophies taught in this book. Jim Rohn used to say, "Learn to be happy with what you have while in pursuit of what you want." That is the ultimate philosophy. Be content along the way while in pursuit of your big dreams. In other words, enjoy the ride! Contentment can be defined as "a state of happiness and satisfaction." Strive daily to be happy and satisfied while still moving toward your goals. Don't wait for some magic day when you finally arrive and allow yourself to enjoy life. Enjoy every step of the way!

Time is by far the most valuable commodity on the planet. It is the great equalizer in life. Both the rich man and the poor man have only so much time. With our owner-finance strategies, we will show you how to build wealth *and* have the time to enjoy life! Building a personal portfolio of notes *is* a business and we want you to view it as such. It is *your* business, and once it is built, it does not require much time to manage. We challenge you to find a superior business model for providing steady long-term passive income than owning a pool of real estate notes.

We have met many workaholic doctors, attorneys, and architects who are miserable and have no vision of how to get off the treadmill. They have built a really nice income, but there is just one big problem: *they are the business* and their life has no style or balance! When you "are the business," everyone wants to speak with *you.* Everyone wants to meet with *you.* You only get paid when *you* do something. All you are doing is *trading time for money.* What a horrible business model! We don't care what their hourly rate is. Many of these people are deceived and think they are wealthy. They are wrong. They may be financially rich, but they are definitely not wealthy. Wealthy people make money whether they are working or not. Hopefully some of these workaholics will discover real estate notes and slowly find a way to get off the treadmill.

Whether you decide to work through all of the steps to create notes or choose to purchase notes, finishing this book will give you the tools and knowledge to begin your wealth journey. We challenge you to break through any mental barriers and block out the negative influences that might prevent you from following through on your life vision. We did it, and so can you. We are just a couple of hardworking guys who stayed focused on the prize. Becoming wealthy is a worthy goal, and we implore you to *go for it!*

> ***"Controlled attention is the act of coordinating all of the faculties of the mind and directing their combined power to a given end. It is an act which can be achieved only by the strictest sort of self-discipline. Learn to fix your attention of a given subject, at will, for whatever length of time you choose. You will have learned the secret to power and plenty! This is concentration. Keep your mind on the things you want and off the things you don't want!"***
>
> —*Napoleon Hill*

WHY SELLER FINANCING? OUR STORY

In the summer of 2009, we were getting our tails kicked by the real estate market. We were primarily focusing on retail flips and we owned about ten properties that we needed to sell. Lenders had really tightened up their underwriting guidelines and it was much harder to find a buyer who could qualify for a loan. Prices were on a downward trend and our homes were just not selling. We decided to lower our selling prices to get them sold ASAP. We broke even on most of the homes and lost a "few bucks" on some of the higher priced homes. Busted! "More than a few bucks"...ouch! We can't tell you the real amount we lost because every time we admit it, we punch a hole in a wall!

We sat on the sidelines with our cash for about six months and ate rice and beans for dinner five nights a week and then decided to go back out into the market and start flipping again. We saw slight improvement in the market so we purchased five homes over the course of sixty days and the "flipping machine" was back online. We knew the market was still tough so we tried to make our homes really stand out by installing granite countertops, stainless-steel appliances, etc. The homes looked fantastic and we thought we had purchased them at great prices to be able to realize a nice profit. We listed the homes for sale in the MLS and waited for buyers to come along and make us offers. We waited…and waited…and waited some more. Four months went by and *not one sale*! At this point we decided to do the same thing as before: sell cheap, cut our losses, go back to eating rice and beans, and redeploy our cash at another time. We sold four of the five homes relatively quickly and actually made a small profit on a couple of the sales.

Now we just had one PIG to get sold. Week after week went by and our $70,000 PIG would just not sell. Finally, out of desperation, I suggested that we try to rent the home so we could start generating income. Erik did not like the idea of having to deal with a tenant so he suggested seller financing the home. Erik was familiar with the seller-finance process because of his past real estate experience. Even though we would be getting our payments one month at a time, we decided to put a sign in the yard that said "SELLER FINANCING." We were tired of having the home sit vacant and just wanted to get it off of our hands.

> "***Listening to pessimistic people makes you unable to hear the sounds of success.***"
>
> —Erik Saengerhausen

In the next twenty-four hours, we got fourteen phone calls, and two days later we had a $10,000 down payment in our hands. We were thrilled it got sold, but at the same time most of our money was tied up and we would be collecting our profit monthly over the next twenty years. At least the PIG was finally starting to produce some income!

A few weeks later, Erik was having dinner with a longtime retired friend named Dick Gueringer. Dick was in his late sixties and living off of the money he had saved and invested over the past thirty years. Dick asked Erik how the real estate business was going, and Erik replied, "It sucks. I even had to offer seller financing on one of the houses in order to get it sold." Erik then asked Dick how his stock investments were doing and Dick replied, "They suck!" They both got a good laugh and then discussed the recent sale we had with seller-financing terms. Erik informed Dick that the buyer agreed to twenty-year financing at 11.9 percent interest. Dick said, "I wish I could get 11.9 percent on my money!" Guess what happened next? We sold our first real estate note!

After selling our first note to Mr. Gueringer, Erik and I looked at each other with a laser-focused stare and said, *let's do it!* As they say…the rest is history. Five years went by and we literally have not looked up until we decided to write this book. The success of our business model has exceeded our expectations. We constantly get asked by other investors how we do it, so we decided to write this book and follow it up with an education course focused on sharing what we have learned while seller financing hundreds of homes and building up a pool of private note buyers. Our education courses can be found at TheNoteFactory.com

Making money in real estate is like putting together the pieces of a puzzle. The typical investor who flips houses has to find a property, hire a contractor to fix it up, and then pay a Realtor to get it sold. That is a relatively straightforward puzzle. The seller-finance puzzle has a few more pieces but when the puzzle is complete, it can be a thing of beauty *and* create unbelievable streams of income and wealth that will last for generations.

Before we get to all of the positive things about the seller-finance business model, we want you to consider some of the challenges associated with this strategy as well:

1. **Licensing:** There have been a lot of changes in the mortgage industry in the past few years and things are continuing to change every year.

Keeping up with the current regulations to ensure you are following the new laws and rules can be somewhat burdensome, to say the least. Currently, if you plan to be in the seller-finance business, you need to be licensed as a Mortgage Loan Originator. (If you are just purchasing notes, no license is required.) There is a cost associated with getting and maintaining your license, and also continuing education is required. Many investors have chosen to deal with the licensing requirement by finding a mortgage company that will provide them with the necessary loan documents to facilitate the transaction instead of getting licensed themselves. Our recommendation is to consult with an attorney who specializes in mortgage law to ensure that you are following state and federal laws.

2. **Servicing Software:** If you are going to do more than a handful of transactions, you will need note-servicing software to accurately keep track of payments. You must be able to account for the amount of principal and interest paid and send a "1098 interest paid" statement each year to all borrowers.
3. **Late payments/potential foreclosure:** Creating long-term streams of income is a beautiful thing. Unfortunately, not every note is going to pay on time, and offering seller financing automatically puts you in the collection business. Most good software packages will produce late notices, and if push comes to shove, you may have to hire an attorney to foreclose on a property. The foreclosure process for each state is different. In Texas, it is a nonjudicial process and relatively quick and inexpensive. Later in this book we will talk more about the strategies we use when dealing with delinquent borrowers.
4. **Escrowing for taxes and insurance:** We escrow for taxes and insurance on all notes that we produce. This helps ensure that property insurance remains in effect and that taxes are paid promptly. The taxes and insurance are collected monthly and should be kept in a separate escrow account. We have heard stories about investors who have gotten themselves into trouble by spending the money they were supposed to be setting aside to pay taxes and insurance. There are some

very specific guidelines that must be followed regarding the amount that can be held in escrow. We will touch on this more in the servicing chapter.

5. **Private investor and banking relationships:** Whether you are going to produce a couple of notes per year or build a $10 million note portfolio, you are going to need "money people." You will need to become the person money people WANT to do business with. Work on your communication skills and be prepared to spend some time building these valuable relationships.

Now that we have discussed some of the challenges with the seller-finance business model, the rest of the chapter is dedicated to explaining why it is *all worth it!*

1. **Owners vs. Renters:** We met a wealthy man recently who asked what we did for a living. We explained that we are in the business of creating and selling real estate notes for ourselves and private investors. During the conversation he told us about a friend who had accumulated more than 150 rental homes during a ten-year period and ended up having to file for bankruptcy! What started out to be a plan to build wealth turned into a financial nightmare!

   We can't tell you how many people we have met in the past ten years who wanted to invest in real estate and chose the rental home route. Almost all of the people we have talked to say something like this: "I used to have rental properties, but I never really made any money and just could not stand the headaches of tenants any longer, so I sold my homes." Even investors who had property management companies often say the same thing. Just because there is a property manager, it does not mean you don't have to write checks for air conditioners, new roofs, and new stoves because the last one got stolen by the previous tenant. We managed our own portfolio of rentals for several years and it went about as well as we could have hoped for. When it was all said and done, we did get some appreciation on our properties, and the tenants did help us pay our mortgages BUT...the routine maintenance and the vacancies between tenants ate up most of the profit. Rarely do we meet anyone who talks about how much money they are making on their rental properties, especially when they have a mortgages on the homes.

When you seller finance a property, the homeowner fixes their own toilet, air conditioner, and leaky kitchen sink. Also, assuming the homeowner keeps paying, the vacancy issue goes away. On a typical rental property, most people collect a deposit in the amount of *one* additional monthly payment. *Big deal!* Most "deposits" are not enough for the tenant to care about when financial trouble comes their way. Let's say we have a house that would rent for $1,000 a month. On a typical rental, most people would collect a $1,000 or even a $2,000 deposit. If you were to owner finance the same property, you would collect about $10,000 from the buyer in the form of a down payment. A buyer who has "skin in the game," is much less likely to flake out when things get a little tough. Most people will beg, borrow, or steal the money to keep a roof over their head if they have $10,000 in the game. Ten thousand dollars has seemed to be the magic number to avoid most payment problems on homes valued under $100,000. If you can't get a solid $10,000 down payment, we would not recommend offering owner-financing terms to a buyer.

2. **Amortization Schedule:** Our friend Joe stopped by our office one day and asked if we would review his paperwork from a house he had financed about ten years earlier from a private seller. We looked over the file and saw that he had paid $65,000 for the house and put $5,000 down. Joe financed $60,000 over thirty years and the interest rate was 10.9 percent. Joe wanted to know how much he still owed. He guessed about $35,000 to $40,000 because he had been paying on the house for ten years.

   When we worked up an amortization schedule for him, we said, "Joe, you still owe a little over $55,000." Joe said "That can't be right! I have been paying on this house for ten years!" We double checked the numbers and verified that they were correct. Joe paid ten years of payments at $566.86 per month for a total of $68,023.20. He only paid $4,717.22 in principal in ten years and he still owed $55,282.78! Read this paragraph again and again. He made payments for ten years and on average paid less than $500 *per year* toward principal. That is the beauty of the amortization schedule, from an investor's perspective. When you offer owner financing, *you* get to collect all of that interest. In the above scenario, you would have collected $63,305.98 in interest during the first ten years of the loan and still be owed $55,282.78 on an original loan of $60,000. If the borrower paid $566.86 for thirty years, they will have paid a total of $204,069.60! Are you starting to see why this business model has such huge potential? Imagine being on the receiving end of multiple streams of income where the vast majority of the money you are receiving is interest!

3. **Appreciation and Principal Pay-Down:** Like a fine wine, as time goes by, a steady-paying note gets better with age. Notes that have been performing for a period of time are called "seasoned" notes. In a "normal" real estate market, if there is such a thing, homes generally appreciate or increase in value over time. As a note is seasoned, the underlying collateral (the home) usually increases in value each year. At the same time, the amount owed on the home gets reduced each year as the homeowner continues to make his monthly payments. The obvious benefit to the note holder is your risk is reduced each year. If the homeowner did quit paying in year seven, for example, the house probably appreciated in value and the original loan balance has been paid down for seven years. This is a double win for the note holder and puts you in a much stronger equity position if you ever needed to foreclose on the property.
4. **Zero Negotiation on Price and Terms:** Back in our days of flipping houses, the one thing we could count on was that either the Realtor, inspector, lender, or appraiser would find a way to throw a wrench into our transaction. The Realtor would try to lowball the offer, or the

inspector would scare the heck out of the new home buyer with his inspection report. Regardless of the situation, we would usually end up discounting the price more than we had planned or end up dealing with more repairs than we hoped for. With seller financing, you are providing so much value for the home buyer that most of those issues just go away. We sell all of our homes *as is* and our interest rate and prices are firm. We lay down the rules of the game up front, and 95 percent of the time there are no issues. When you offer owner financing, you make the rules.

5. **Supply and Demand:** There are more buyers looking for owner-financing opportunities than there is supply in most cities. The mistake most rookie investors make is that they take the first warm body that shows up and is willing to give them a down payment. Remember, you are trying to create headache-free, long-term streams of income. We will teach you how to find the right buyer in our chapter "Character Underwriting." For now, realize that there is a huge demand for seller financing, and the wise investor patiently waits for the "right buyer" to come along. Think of it like getting married: it is better to wait to find the right person before you rush to the altar.
6. **Bringing Value to the Community:** Oftentimes when we purchase a home, the neighbors come over and start talking to us. They want to know what we are going to do with the house. When we tell them that we are going to fix up the property, they are ecstatic! Many of our homes have been the ugly duckling on the street for a long time. They also ask if we plan to rent the home or sell it. You should see their faces light up when we tell them we are going to sell the home and not rent it. The neighbors love to know they are going to have someone in the house with pride of ownership, not a rotating supply of tenants.

Seller financing is the best way we have discovered to get on the path to creating passive streams of income and true wealth. Now let's get down to business and go find your first home!

ERIK AND MIKE'S BOTTOM LINE:
There is huge demand for seller financing. Become an expert creating quality real estate notes, as it is one of the surest ways to wealth building ever discovered.

"Personal initiative bears the same relationship to an individual that a starter bears to an automobile! It is the power that starts all action. It is the power that assures completion of anything one begins. Personal initiative is the inner power that starts all action. It is the dynamo that spurs the faculty of your imagination into action and inspires you to finish what you start. Personal initiative is self-motivation."

—Napoleon Hill

4

TREASURE HUNT

By now, hopefully you are excited about the idea of building passive income and getting on the road to creating wealth. Knowing that something is a good idea and has amazing potential is one thing; taking action is another. Knowledge is *not* power. Knowledge put into *action* is power. Each chapter of this book will give you one more piece of knowledge, but will only pay dividends if you take action. We will lead you to the well of knowledge and skill, but it's up to you to drink. Having only four of the five numbers needed to open the combination lock will not do the job. Stay the course and keep reading to unlock the vault of endless streams of income.

Searching for properties is one of the most enjoyable and exciting steps in the real estate game. It truly is an adrenaline rush when you go on your treasure hunt and find a property, make an offer, and get it under contract. The thrill of the hunt never gets old. We both are consistently searching for properties and always try to show each other up by snagging the best deal of the week.

Our goal with this chapter is to point you in the right direction on your property treasure hunt. Generally speaking, we like to focus on established lower-price neighborhoods. We target the lowest priced areas that still look and feel stable. Most cities have stable, low-price areas along with areas that are in decline. There is often a fine line between what constitutes a good owner-finance area and a bad area. When in doubt, only buy homes in areas that you are comfortable with. Our philosophy in a nutshell is to buy homes in lower-price areas where good, hardworking people would want to live. In other words, make sure the home you buy will attract a quality buyer when it's fixed up and ready to sell.

Here are some of the key things to look for when you begin your treasure hunt:

WHAT TO HUNT FOR

Established Neighborhood

What is an established neighborhood? An established neighborhood is an area where there are more homeowners than renters and one that tends to be very stable. As we previously mentioned, the goal is to buy a house that will attract a quality buyer, and quality buyers like to live in stable neighborhoods. Have you ever driven down a street and had the feeling that nobody takes care of their homes on this block? Chances are the block might be full of rental properties or government-subsidized housing. Avoid buying homes in these areas.

The goal is to target homes for purchase in areas that show pride of ownership. "Pride of ownership" is a phrase we use to describe a home that has been well-maintained. Usually the yard looks neat and manicured, the paint looks fresh, and the overall impression of the home is that it has been well taken care of. Contrast that vision with two cars parked on the front lawn, a couch and refrigerator on the front porch, and two fierce-looking dogs chained to the tree in the front yard. Get the picture?

About a year ago, we bought a home in an established area and were confident we had purchased a great property at a fantastic price. We went "all out" on the rehab and installed all new electrical wiring, central heat, new kitchen cabinets, and a new roof. Usually homes like that sell in the first thirty days, but this one took more than a year! Why? The neighbor from hell—that's why! It turns out that the next-door neighbor worked on hot rod cars in the evenings and on weekends. Engines were revving and power tools were screaming at literally all hours of the night. There was no way we were going to sell our house with all of that noise next door. We contacted the city to complain, but nothing was ever done. Eventually, the neighbor got evicted and we sold our house within a week.

We learned a very expensive and valuable lesson that you should try to avoid at all costs: you absolutely have to be aware of your surroundings when purchasing a house, especially your immediate neighbors. Once you get a home under contract, drive by the house in the evening and on the weekend to make sure there is nothing crazy going on near your home. Barking dogs have cost us thousands over the years. We literally have had to lower the prices on some of our homes in order to get them sold due to the neighbor's dog! Pay attention to what's going on next door to the house you are considering buying!

Curb Appeal

We like to purchase homes with good curb appeal or that have the potential to have good curb appeal. If we find a house that we want to purchase, we try to visualize exactly what we would do in order to give it great curb appeal. Good curb appeal equals a fast sale. Oftentimes, it is as simple as trimming the trees so you can better see the house, planting some shrubs, pressure-washing the house, painting the exterior, installing shutters, or painting the front door.

The homes you want to avoid are the ones that have no hope of ever looking "sexy" from the curb. Stay away from homes with ugly weekend-warrior additions, flat gravel roofs, steep driveways, or anything else that is too difficult or next to impossible to correct. Curb appeal can also be affected by what is located near your property. Avoid homes located next to commercial properties, and, once again, pay close attention to your immediate neighbors.

An ugly house or a commercial property next door can hurt your sale, but a beautiful home next door sure can help! We have bought many homes that were nestled between some of the nicest homes on the block and they always sold quickly and for top dollar. Pay attention to the neighbors; they can help you or hurt you depending on the condition of their property.

Size Matters

We don't like to buy any houses smaller than one thousand square feet, and we prefer homes with at least three bedrooms. We have found that small houses with only two bedrooms seem to attract the "wrong" type of buyer and take much longer to sell. Larger homes with at least three bedrooms tend to attract married couples with children, and these buyers, in our experience, have been our most stable payers. Three-bedroom homes simply appeal to a larger percentage of the population. With two-bedroom homes, you are limiting your pool of prospective buyers and are less likely to attract families.

> ***"Don't let your learning lead to knowledge. Let your learning lead to action."***
>
> —*Jim Rohn*

Layout

Almost every time we have had trouble selling a house it is due to one of two things: it was either too small or the home had a "funky" layout. We have literally purchased hundreds of homes, and you would be surprised at how many times we have overlooked layout issues that have cost us thousands to deal with. Don't ask us what some of the architects were smoking when they designed some of these homes, but rest assured, if you end up getting stuck with an unconventional floorplan, it will eat into your profit and be tough to sell.

Let's start with the living room. Make sure it has enough space to fit furniture for a "normal"-size family. One lawn chair and a TV won't cut it. We can't tell you how many times we have purchased a nice-size home at great price and then struggle to sell it due to the size of the living room. You may ask yourself how seasoned investors could miss something so obvious. We typically look at more than one hundred properties per week and don't always have the luxury of spending the amount of time we would ideally like to analyze each house properly. Oftentimes the houses are full of furniture, and we are dodging kids and pets while making our quick walk through the home. It is also common to have multiple investors looking at a property at the same time, which can distract us and keep us from focusing on the task at hand.

Make sure the kitchen is functional as well. You would be surprised how many times we have purchased homes and then started the renovation process only to realize there was not a place for either a stove or refrigerator. A lot of the homes we purchase are fifty, sixty, or even seventy years old. Somewhere along the way, overly enthusiastic homeowners remodel their kitchens to add cabinets and counter space and I guess they moved the fridge or stove into the living room. Hey, something has to give right? What's more important, counter space or cold beer? Everyone has different priorities!

Closet space has been a deal killer for us as well. People tend to need a heck of a lot more closet space than they did fifty years ago. Make sure each bedroom has its own closet and that the master bedroom closet is a good size. If the closet in the master is very small, see if the bedroom is large enough to build a larger closet without making the bedroom too small.

You also want to ensure that all bedrooms have their own entrance. We have bought houses that have "three bedrooms," but you have to walk through one bedroom to get to the other. Nobody wants to have their bedroom used as a "hallway." You would think these issues would be obvious, but when you are looking at the house for the first time, you'd be amazed at how much you might overlook. Take your time when first viewing the property. We recommend always starting at the front door and walking the house in a very systematic way. Open every door, check the closets, inspect the bathrooms, and visualize the location of the appliances and where the furniture will be positioned.

It is also a good idea to take a few pictures and make some notes on each property that you are considering making an offer on. This will help you remember most of the issues you will be dealing with and also give you some ammo when trying to negotiate a lower purchase price with a seller.

Here's why you might miss things on the first walk-through.

Try to read the paragraph below, then consider what it actually says.

The brain is a wonderful thing, isn't it?
Aoccdrng to rscheearch at Cmabridge Uinervtisy, it deosnt mttaer in what oredr the ltteers in a word are, the olny iprmoetnt tihng is that the frist and lsat ltteer be in the rghit pclae. The rset can be a total mses and you can sltil raed it wouthit porbelm. This is bcuseae the huamn mnid deos not raed ervey lteter by istlef, but the word as a wlohe and the biran fguiers it out aynaway. WOW!

The same thing applies when looking at a house. Our brain tell us, yes, that is a bedroom. What it doesn't tell us is that the bedroom is too small or there is no door, closet, or window. That is why we suggest walking in and out a couple of times so our brains can "reset" and be aware of any floorplan issues. Even the smallest distraction can cause you to overlook something and cost you thousands.

"Self-discipline, or self-control, means taking possession of your own mind.

HOW TO HUNT

Now that you know what the treasure looks like, let's get ready to go hunting. Finding a great deal and getting it under contract is an exhilarating feeling, but it takes work. Patience and perseverance are key to your success. Most of the best deals are not listed in the MLS system and finding them can be challenging. Wouldn't it be great to be able to call a Realtor and say, "Find me a great deal way under market value"? We wish it were that easy. Realtors can definitely help you in your search, but remember, every Realtor in town has access to the same real estate listings, and the competition for listed properties is fierce. Pick out a few of the strategies listed below that you are comfortable with and persevere until you start finding deals.

Driving for Dollars

Sounds simple doesn't it? In our opinion, it is the best and least expensive way to find houses when you first start investing. Pick out a specific neighborhood and drive the streets looking for vacant houses and also homes that look like they have been neglected. Look for things like broken or boarded-up windows, unmowed grass, peeling paint, and roofs that look shot. Write down the street address and do a search on your local county appraisal district website.

You will find that there are usually two addresses. One is the address to the actual house and the other is the mailing address for the tax bill. If they are *different*, you are probably dealing with an absentee owner, and your odds of buying the house just went up significantly. Absentee owners of dilapidated properties tend to be highly motivated sellers since it's not their homestead and apparently they don't have the time or money to make repairs. Oftentimes these properties are old rentals, inherited homes, or investment projects gone bad. If there are two addresses, mail a letter to the address where the tax bill is being sent. This letter should ask the owner if he is interested in selling the property. Let him know you are a *cash* buyer and can close quickly. We consistently buy homes using this strategy. Here is a sample letter:

ALAMO
HOME SOURCE

Dear Mr. and Mrs. Ortiz,

I was driving by your home yesterday at 11511 Hatchet Pass and thought I would send you this brief letter. I pay CASH for homes and literally have helped hundreds of San Antonio residents over the past 10 years. I am known as San Antonio's number one source for CASH home purchases with no headaches.

If you would consider selling your home, please call me today at 210-439-4471. My name is Erik Saengerhausen and I purchase homes AS-IS and do not require any inspections, appraisals, or surveys. I pay 100% of all closing costs and will provide you proof of funds at the time we sign a contract. I have a real estate license but am not interested in listing your home. I just want to purchase it for CASH.

There are a lot of so called "investors" that play games and promise you the stars and moon but DO NOT DELIVER. I am the real deal and will give you NON-REFUNDABLE earnest money and can usually close within three days.

Your neighbors will thank you for selling the home to us. We will renovate the property and DO NOT RENT any of the homes that we purchase. We only sell to well qualified San Antonio residents.
Enclosed is a $1.00 down payment towards the purchase of your home. If you are ready to sell today, please call me immediately at

210-439-4471. If not, please buy yourself a soda on me and save my business card for future reference.
May God continue to bless you and your family.

Sincerely,
Erik Saengerhausen

One other way to increase your odds while driving for dollars is to take the time to speak to the neighbors and ask them the "story" of the house. More often than not, someone will be willing to share information about the owner. Try to get the contact information from the neighbor and be sure to leave them yours. If you are unable to connect with the neighbors, put a big neon orange sticker on the front door that says "I Buy Houses for Cash" with your phone number. We have had a great response from these stickers. Even if the home is vacant, usually someone is checking on the house or the "nosy neighbor" will see the sticker and relay the information to the owner. Driving for dollars is one of the best ways to find houses at any stage of your investment career. We still drive for dollars and always will. Develop the habit of cruising your target neighborhoods with pen in hand whenever you have some extra time. Here is a sample of one of our stickers we use regularly.

ATTENTION

We have made numerous attempts to contact you

PLEASE CALL ERIK SAENGERHAUSEN IMMEDIATELY AT 210-439-4471

ONE OF YOUR NIEGHBORS REACHED OUT TO US AND ASKED IF WE WOULD CONTACT YOU REGARDING THE POSSIBLE SALE OF THE PROPERTY.

WE OFFER FAST – FAIR – CASH OFFERS & CAN CLOSE IN 7 DAYS OR LESS

PLEASE CALL ERIK SAENGERHAUSEN IMMEDIATELY AT 210-439-4471

One thing you will quickly discover about the real estate business is that you will be spending a lot of time in your vehicle. Some of the best advice we ever got from our mentor, Mr. Rohn, was to turn your vehicle into a mobile library. Load up your phone or iPod with a bunch of quality audiobooks. Focus on things that will help educate you and improve your skills. You can "read" a few good books a month if you get in the habit of shutting off the radio and listening to a good audiobook.

The Newspaper

Your local newspaper will have many ads with houses for sale, but that's not what you are looking for. You are looking for the investors who are running ads to *buy* houses. Go to the "Homes for Sale" page and you should see a section with ads that say "We Buy Houses." Call those investors and introduce yourself. Let them know you are an investor who has cash and can close quickly. Ask if they have any houses in your target areas that they are willing to sell. Many people running ads in the paper are wholesalers who need "real" investors with cash to buy the houses they get under contract. You should get to know every wholesaler in your city and nurture those relationships. Ask them to contact you first when they are looking to wholesale a property and tell them that you move fast. Take them to lunch on a regular basis. You can purchase a lot of houses from wholesalers if you take the time to build their trust and confidence. Wholesalers are often working under very tight deadlines and need cash investors who move fast and can close on the deal ASAP.

You should also place an ad in the newspaper. Just a simple "We Buy Houses" ad with your phone number is all you need. This is a relatively inexpensive way to get the phone to ring and has been quite effective for us. In many larger cities like San Antonio, Texas, there are often several smaller publications that serve specific parts of the city. Do your homework and find out which publication is targeting the areas where you want to buy homes and place your ads there.

Mailings

Postcards are a great way to target a specific neighborhood or an entire city. We would suggest sticking to a specific neighborhood or a certain group of ZIP codes and "blast" it once a month for six to twelve months. Our experience has shown that it takes multiple impressions to get results. Our average response rate has been about 1 percent, but we have made some very profitable deals from our mailing campaigns. If we mail out five thousand postcards, we usually receive about fifty calls. Out of those fifty calls we may look at only ten to fifteen houses and make one or two deals. If you can't stay the course for at least six months, don't spend the money. History has proven that it is the repetition that gets the results.

When it comes to the size of the postcard, we suggest jumbo, which is 8.5" by 5.5". Pick out a bright color that will catch someone's eye when they open the mailbox. Have a headline that will keep their attention. Then get to the point immediately. It should take less than three seconds to sell them. Remember, KISS: *Keep It Simple, Stupid.* Postcard campaigns can yield good results, but it takes a significant financial commitment. If you are just starting out, some of our other strategies might be a better place to start.

Build Your Own Website

You can set up your own "We Buy Houses" website to attract people looking to sell their houses. There are several companies that offer affordable website templates geared toward real estate investors. Check out www.LeadPropeller.com. We know several investors who have had fantastic results working with this company.

The competition among "We Buy Houses" websites is tough, and you really need to know what you are doing if you expect to get any results. We are not experts in this area and prefer to use some of our other strategies for finding properties. We do know that if you are going to use Google AdWords and pay-per-click advertising, you better know what you are doing or it could cost you a small fortune.

Craigslist

Craigslist is a great way to find houses for sale. Go to your city and search "Homes for Sale by Owner." Do not search by "broker" or you will get hundreds of homes for sale by Realtors. Many motivated sellers advertise their homes on Craigslist because they don't want to pay real estate commissions or they don't have a lot of time to sell. These sellers need a cash buyer who can close fast. The key to getting results from Craigslist is to have the discipline to look at it on a very consistent basis and move fast. Good deals don't last long.

Many investors also post properties they want to wholesale on Craigslist. Once again, consistency is key. Time is of the essence when a hot lead gets posted. Also, you should run your own "I BUY HOUSES" ad and post a new ad daily so you are always near the top of the list. With Craigslist, the price is right: FREE!

HUD Foreclosure Website

All HUD (Housing and Urban Development) homes, which are FHA foreclosures, are posted on www.HUDHOMESTORE.com. This is a very user-friendly site and it is easy to search for homes in your area. You do need a licensed Realtor to submit an offer, but you can view the homes online and do a preliminary drive-by prior to calling your Realtor. Many HUD homes are sold exclusively to homeowners (not investors) for the first thirty days the home is listed for sale. This is frustrating for investors, but the lesson here is to be ready to make your offer on day thirty-one if the home is still available!

Courthouse Steps

In Texas, the first Tuesday of the month there is an auction on the courthouse steps of the county in which the property is located. This is potentially one of the best ways to get a good deal but also one of the riskiest. The reason it can be risky is because there is no title insurance, and most of the time you did not have the opportunity to view the inside of the property. Also, many properties purchased on the courthouse steps are occupied and you may have to file an eviction suit to get the occupants to leave. These issues, along with potential back taxes and IRS liens, make this a very high-risk way for a rookie investor to acquire a property.

Our recommendation is that you sit down with a real estate attorney to help educate you on the process prior to trying to purchase a property at a foreclosure auction. Once you learn the ropes, bring a pocket full of money and be ready to buy. A word of caution: just because a house is a foreclosure does not mean it is a good deal. Every time we are at the auction we see some new investor massively overpaying for properties. Do your homework and proceed with caution. In most large cities, there are companies that research all of the homes posted for foreclosure and sell the list to investors. If you get serious about pursuing foreclosures, this information is well worth the small subscription price.

Many investors have learned very expensive and valuable lessons trying to buy foreclosures. One time we purchased a house through the MLS and a few days into the rehab an investor came to the house and told our contractor to pack up his tools because we were working on *his* house. Our contractor called us immediately and we drove to the house right away to discuss the situation. He was yelling at us when we got out of the truck and was waving his deed in our faces. Sure enough, his deed was for the same *physical* address as our house. What the rookie investor did not realize is that the *legal* address was different. When we studied his paperwork, we explained to him that he had actually purchased the vacant lot *next* to our house. He paid $42,000 for a lot that was worth about $10,000. His face turned white and he quietly walked to his truck and drove away. When you buy on the courthouse steps, there is no title insurance and no refunds. Buyer, beware!

Bird Dogs

A bird dog is basically someone you teach how to drive around for you to help you find properties. It is the same premise as our Driving for Dollars strategy except someone else is doing the driving. This is perfect for someone looking to make some extra money such as a college student or a retired person. We pay them about $500 if we end up buying a home that they find. We always ask them to e-mail us a picture of the property along with a picture of the houses next door. We like to get a feel for the area before we invest the time to actually drive by the property.

Bandit Signs

Bandit signs are nothing more than handwritten signs that you put up in the neighborhoods where you want to buy. We write "I BUY HOUSES" and our phone number and that's it. In many cities, you can get fined if you nail a sign to a telephone pole so we put our signs up on small metal stands that easily push into ground. We drive up and down several streets looking for strategic locations to place our signs. Vacant lots, grocery store exits, and Walmart parking lots are some of our favorite spots. We even sneak a few signs in the yards of homes listed by other Realtors. (Make sure they are vacant!) Try to avoid areas where your signs will be taken down easily by kids or code compliance personnel. Putting up signs is a bit of a cat-and-mouse game and they tend to disappear fast. As long as we are not putting up too many signs in one specific area, we don't hear any complaints from neighbors or city officials. Keep your signs spread out over a number of different streets and be sure to research the rules and regulations for signage in your specific city. Some cities require you to actually purchase a sign permit. Try to play by the rules in your local area.

Don't underestimate the power of bandit signs. We consistently put up signs and consistently buy properties. One strategy that we use regularly is to put up signs at 4:00 a.m. on a Saturday morning. Try it! It is tough to get out of bed, but you will feel like a high school kid who snuck out of your bedroom window to go have some fun, AND there is a good chance you will get a call to buy a house that weekend! Have fun with your signs too. Here are two that we made a couple of years ago and had an absolute blast with. The phone definitely rings with these signs.

MLS

The Multiple Listing Service, MLS for short, is the obvious place to look for properties and the vast majority of homes listed for sale are found here. This is where most Realtors list their clients' homes for sale. Banks and other lending institutions also hire Realtors to list their foreclosed properties on the MLS. The downside to the MLS is that every buyer in the market is looking at the same properties as you. The competition is fierce and you will need to move fast when you come across a hot property.

Find a Realtor who works in the area you want to target. Drive these neighborhoods and call several of the Realtors who have homes for sale in the area. Set up a face-to-face meeting with multiple Realtors and let them know you are new to the business but serious about investing. Communicate that you are looking for a Realtor who is readily available to show homes, pull comparable sales, and submit offers promptly. Many Realtors are only part-time and work other jobs. Be sure that the Realtor you choose is a full-time real estate professional. Don't settle for subpar service from a Realtor. In most large cities there are thousands of licensed Realtors to choose from. Choose wisely and make sure you are confident the Realtor is the right partner for you.

Most Realtors have the ability to set up an automatic e-mail notification whenever a new listing hits the market in your target area and price range. Get into a habit of checking these e-mails promptly and doing an initial "drive by" prior to calling your Realtor. Only get your Realtor involved after you have decided you definitely want to get inside the home. The pictures might look good on the MLS; however, when you drive by, the house might be located in a rough area or have a neighbor from hell. Don't waste your Realtor's time. Ask them to show you houses only when you have done some preliminary homework and think it might be a good investment.

We know many investors who buy exclusively off the MLS and make a great living. If you rely solely on the MLS, be prepared to make a lot of offers and move quickly—due to the extreme competition.

Now that you think you've found a treasure, let's seal the deal and get it under contract!

ERIK AND MIKE'S BOTTOM LINE:
Patience, patience, patience. You make money in real estate when you BUY. When you are first starting out, buy very straightforward renovation projects. Once you purchase a home, you are married to it. Buying a property under market value is the most crucial step in the entire note-creation process. On your first few deals, get some help crunching the numbers from a Realtor or another investor to make sure you will end up with a profitable deal.

"Creative vision is a quality of mind belonging only to men and women who follow the habit of going the extra mile, for it recognizes no such thing as the regularity of working hours, is not concerned with monetary compensation, and its highest aim is to do the impossible.

"Creative vision is definitely and closely related to that state of mind known as faith, and it is significant that those who have demonstrated the greatest amount of creative vision are known to have been men with a great capacity for faith. This is both logical and understandable when we recognize that faith is the means of approach to Infinite Intelligence, the source of all knowledge and all facts, both great and small.

"The imagination is the workshop of the soul wherein are shaped all plans for individual achievement."

—*Napoleon Hill*

5

GETTING YOUR OFFERS ACCEPTED

The real estate market is imperfect and quirky, to say the least. The list price is not always the best indicator of market value. There are many uneducated sellers and inexperienced Realtors who do a poor job pricing their properties. Oftentimes the list price is ridiculously high, and sometimes it is well below market value. Every seller has a unique reason for selling and a different level of motivation. Your job as a savvy real estate investor is to make sure you stay in tune with the market and educate yourself on property values in the areas where you want to buy. You do this by having your Realtor consistently show you homes and keep you updated on what they are selling for. Once you get in tune with home values, you will be able to recognize a good deal and move quickly to snag it.

DETERMINING YOUR MAXIMUM PURCHASE PRICE

Before we get into the key strategies we use to consistently purchase properties below market value, you must determine three things in order to determine your maximum purchase price:

1. **Determine the ARV.** This stands for "after-repair value." This is the projected sales price/market value of the home after the renovations are made. All Realtors have the ability to easily determine market value by looking at historical sales data in the MLS. This data will show what homes have been selling for on a "price per square foot" basis in the immediate area.

2. **Target profit.** Obviously, most investors would like this to be as high as possible, but market conditions often dictate the amount of profit that can realistically be made. Our philosophy is to make a reasonable profit and sell our homes quickly at market value.
3. **Estimated cost of repairs to make the home marketable.** In the following chapter on rehabbing, we go into detail on how to determine your renovation budget. We also explain why it is much easier to stick to your budget while renovating a seller-financed home compared to a flip property. For now, we just want you to understand the formula for dialing in your maximum purchase price.

The formula for determining what you can pay for a home is simple:

ARV - [TARGET PROFIT + COST OF REPAIRS] = MAXIMUM PURCHASE PRICE

Along with determining our maximum purchase price, we always ask ourselves the following two questions before making a formal written offer. If the answer is yes to these two questions, we go forward with our offer:

1. If we sell this house for market value, can we create a note that will deliver a double-digit return to our note buyers and still realize a reasonable profit?
2. If we sell this home for market value, can we pledge the note for collateral with our bank and get 100 percent of our invested working capital back *and* have positive cash flow?

One of the key factors to getting a "yes" to question number one regarding delivering a "double-digit" return to a note buyer is to know what homes are renting for in the same area as the house you are considering buying. In order to create a marketable note, we want the interest rate to be at least 10 percent and *still* have the payment about the same as rents in the area. Most buyers are concerned about their monthly payment and *not* necessarily the interest rate.

If they are renting a home for $1,000 a month and can buy their own home for about the same payment, most buyers couldn't care less if the interest rate is 2 percent or 12 percent. They care about their monthly payment.

When we sell homes, we have found that we can charge 10 percent interest or more on lower priced homes under $100,000 but not necessarily on higher priced homes. The higher the sales price, the larger the discrepancy between the monthly payments and market rent. To better illustrate this point, take a look at the following two homes both financed with the exact same terms: 10 percent down, thirty-year financing at 10.9 percent interest, and take note of how the monthly payment compares to renting a home in the same price range.

$100,000 home
10 percent down payment
$90,000 loan for thirty years
Principal and interest monthly payment at 10.9 percent: $850.30
Market rent for a $100K house: $1,000–$1,200

$500,000 home
10 percent down payment
$450,000 loan for thirty years
Principal and interest monthly payment at 10.9 percent: $4,251.49
Market rent for a $500K house: $2,500-$2,800

As you can see, the monthly payment on the $500,000 house is significantly higher than the cost to rent a similar home. This is why we target lower priced homes. The payment for the family who purchased the $100,000 house actually went *down* compared to their rent. Even if we add taxes and insurance to their payment, the total monthly payment is still going to be about the same or less than they were paying to rent. Keeping the payments about the same as rent while still charging 10 percent interest or more is one of the major keys to creating solid marketable notes. We have found that note buyers generally expect a yield of 10 percent or more, and we can deliver those yields if we focus on buying the lower priced homes in the city.

Many people who buy our homes can't qualify for a traditional mortgage for any number of reasons. They just don't fit into the traditional mortgage box and get rejected continuously from traditional banks and mortgage companies. It might be that they are self-employed, new to the country, or just don't have a high enough credit score or any credit at all. What choices do these folks have? Rent forever? Many wonderful people can't qualify for a traditional loan but have a significant down payment and make good income. Our job is to find these people and provide them an alternative financing opportunity. These families are extremely grateful for the financing opportunity and the fact that they are paying 10 percent interest or higher is usually a nonissue. The interest rate charged is reasonable due to the additional risk associated with these types of borrowers. When we finance a home, we let the buyer know that the interest rate is fixed and they can refinance anytime and not suffer a prepayment penalty.

Regarding the term "reasonable profit," everyone defines it differently. If you are living at home with your parents and working out of a bedroom, making a quick $10,000 can be huge. If you have to pay for employees and office space, you may need a larger profit margin to cover your overhead. This is one of the beautiful things about real estate investing. The small individual investor can tiptoe into the market and make some really nice profits while keeping his or her expenses extremely low.

For us, "reasonable profit" is greatly influenced by the amount of work and time we have to spend getting the home ready to sell. We might be willing to take a smaller profit if we can get the home back on the market within a week, for example. Another factor we consider when determining our maximum purchase price is the current demand for our real estate notes. Oftentimes we have note buyers "standing in line" and we may be willing to pay more for a property and take less of a profit in order to create notes quickly to satisfy demand. The faster we sell our notes, the faster we get our working capital back. This allows us to "turn" our money multiple times a year and increase our overall profits.

Study the numbers below on the *buy* and *sell* side of transactions that we do every day to get a better understanding of how the numbers shake out on a typical deal.

TYPICAL "BUY" TRANSACTION:

Home List Price: $100,000
After Repair Value: $120,000
Target Gross Profit: $25,000
Estimated Repairs Needed: $15,000
Maximum Purchase Price: $80,000 ($120K ARV - [$25K profit +$15K repairs] = $80K)

Let's say we were able to purchase the home for $80,000, do the renovations, and put it back on the market for sale. Here is how the numbers typically shake out:

TYPICAL "SELL" TRANSACTION:

Sales Price After Rehab: $120,000
Down Payment Collected: $15,000
Loan Amount/Note Created: $105,000
Interest Rate: 10.9 percent
Loan Term: 30 years
Monthly Payment: $992.01 (principal and interest)
Total Investment In This Real Estate Transaction: $80,000
(Purchase price of $80K + $15K rehab - $15K down payment received from home buyer)

Study those numbers again; we just created a $105,000 real estate note with 10.9 percent interest and have a total investment of only $80,000!

Plus, if the homeowner makes all of their scheduled payments, we will receive a total of $357,123.60! Not bad for an $80,000 investment.

Now, back to our first question: *If we sell this house for market value, can we deliver a double-digit return to our note buyers and still realize a reasonable profit? Yes*! If we sold the note to an investor at face value ($105,000), we would realize a profit of $25,000, and the note buyer/investor would receive a double-digit return of 10.9 percent! If you chose to increase the yield to above 10.9 percent to your note buyer, you could "discount the note."

Discounting a note is defined as "selling a note for a price lower than face value." For example, you could sell your note buyer a $105,000 note for $100,000 or even $95,000 and still make a nice profit. Take a look at the following discounted note examples to get a clearer understanding of the concept of discounting notes.

$105,000 note at 10.9 percent sold for $105,000 (sold at face value), yield to investor: 10.9 percent
$105,000 note at 10.9 percent sold for $100,000 ($5,000 discount), yield to investor: 11.52 percent
$105,000 note at 10.9 percent sold for $95,000 ($10,000 discount), yield to investor: 12.2 percent
$105,000 note at 10.9 percent sold for $90,000 ($15,000 discount), yield to investor: 12.95 percent

As you see in the example above, the more you discount a note, the higher the yield to the note buyer. Obviously, your profit is reduced by the direct amount of the note discount. Our "sweet spot" to get private investors to stand in line for our notes has been 10 to 12 percent yields. If you present a note with a solid down payment and a 10 percent to 12 percent yield, investors will have a hard time saying "no" to that income stream.

Let's take a look at the second question we asked earlier: *If we sell this home for market value, can we pledge the note for collateral with our bank and get 100 percent of our invested working capital back* and *have positive cash flow?*

Yes! Most banks are willing to lend about 80 percent of the value of the note. In the example above, the note was created for $105,000. If the bank lends us 80 percent of the value of the note, they would lend $84,000 ($105,000 x 0.8 = $84,000). Our total investment was only $80,000. We could borrow only the $80,000 or borrow $84,000 and put the $4,000 in our pocket.

When we pledge a note as collateral and borrow money from a bank, we like to borrow on a fixed interest rate for a ten-year term. As of the writing of this book, we are paying between 5.5 percent and 6 percent. Let's take a look at how the cash flows:

Payment being made by buyer: $992.01 (thirty-year loan at 10.9 percent)
Payment due to the bank: $868.21($80,000 loan for ten years at 5.5 percent)

As you see in this example, we got all of our working capital back *and* have positive cash flow. If this homeowner paid as agreed for the full term of the note, after ten years the bank will be paid off and the borrower will still owe us $96,744.86! If the borrower sells the home or refinances, we will get paid off and have all of our cash back to do it again. If the borrower quits making payments, we can foreclose and get the house back, collect a new down payment, and sell it again. Our experience with notes has been this: any way things go, we end up making money! Can you say that about stocks, bonds, or oil wells? Heck no! Notes *rock*!

INCREASING YOUR "SNAG" RATE

To drastically increase the odds of your offer being accepted, use the following key strategies and your "snagged it" rate will go through the roof! We have included some sample dialogue that we use when communicating with Realtors and sellers. The goal is to incorporate some or all of these strategies into the buying process to increase your odds of successfully purchasing a property under market value.

1. **Move fast!** We buy a *huge* percentage of our homes simply because we move quickly. When a new listing hits the market or there is a price reduction in our target area, we immediately look at the homes and make offers if we think we might be able to make a deal. Price reductions are a key indicator you might be dealing with a motivated seller. Some sellers *need* to sell quickly, and Realtors often lower the price every week or so until it gets sold. Be prepared to pounce when you see a price reduction. It may be getting real close to being a great deal.

   Moving fast not only means preparing the offer quickly, it also means creating a sense of urgency with your Realtor and the listing agent. Remember, you don't have a solid deal until you have a signed contract. We have lost out on hundreds of homes by being too darn slow at making our offer. The minute we decide to make an offer, we call the listing Realtor and say something like this: "Hi, John, I looked at the house you have listed at 123 Main Street and wanted to give you a heads up that I have a cash offer coming your way within the next thirty minutes. I would greatly appreciate you presenting my offer to the seller this afternoon and let me know if they will accept it."

   After we send the offer, usually via e-mail, we always make a follow-up call: "John, I just e-mailed you the offer and wanted to make sure you received it. I will be available all afternoon and will be waiting for your call. I am chasing a few other properties, but your listing is my first choice. Please contact me as soon as you speak with your seller to let me know if we have a deal." If we don't hear anything within a reasonable time, we start texting the Realtor for updates. Some people might view this as being "pushy," but, remember, you are the one with the *cash*, and the prize often goes to the one who gets out of the gate first. Keep pushing until you know whether or not you have a deal.

2. **Don't try to steal it!** Early in our real estate investing days, we would run all over town making "lowball" offers and just waste a bunch of time and energy. The refinement to the philosophy is to give your best offer up front and present it as "firm." This simple strategy has helped us get a very high percentage of our offers accepted within hours of presenting them. Most investors make really low offers and then hope to negotiate their way to their target "buy" price. There is a lot of competition in the marketplace, and by the time they are done playing games, someone else comes in and snags the property at a fair price.

    Whether we are dealing directly with a homeowner or a licensed real estate agent, the verbal presentation of the offer goes something like this: "Hi, John, I just e-mailed you the offer on 123 Main Street. I offered $74,000, which is a very fair price from a *cash* investor due to the condition of the property. Seventy-four thousand dollars is the most that I am willing to pay. Most investors initially submit lowball offers; however, I am extremely busy and don't want to waste your time with a ridiculous offer. I always put the highest price I am willing to pay on the table up front."

    We truly are after a win-win negotiation. We have found that price is not the only thing that is important to a seller. Oftentimes they just need the certainty that they have a solid buyer who can move fast, and as long as the price is in the ballpark, they will often accept our offer. Your job, or your Realtor's job if you are being represented, is to help persuade the seller or seller's agent to view the offer as a win-win deal by using all of these strategies to help make the offer more attractive to the seller. Once again, price is not always the primary motivation for all sellers. They are often just looking for certainty: a solid clean offer so they can get on with their lives.

3. **No contingencies**. Most real estate courses and Realtors will tell you to be sure to get an "option period" or "feasibility period" in the contract. The idea behind the option period is to give you time to inspect the home to know exactly what you are purchasing. For rookie investors, this is a good idea. Once you know the game, you may be able to snag properties at a much lower price and faster if you present your offer without an option period or any other contingencies. In other words, no contingencies and no option period means you are willing to buy the house *as is*. Sellers love the idea of selling a home *as is* for *cash* and will often accept a lower price with these conditions.

   Obviously there is some additional risk by not getting the house formally inspected. If we see something in a home that greatly concerns us, we will ask for an option period and get the home inspected. We focus on buying lower priced, basic, affordable homes, and most of the repairs needed are quite obvious. Use this tool carefully, but when you are confident you know what you are buying, present your offer with no contingencies and no option period and you will snag many more properties below market value.
4. **Fast closing dates**. Usually the sooner the closing date the sexier the offer is to the seller, especially if the home is vacant. On a cash offer, Texas title companies can usually get a contract closed in three or four days. We usually draw up our closing dates for five business days after we submit the offer. Realtors and sellers *love* the fact that the deal will be closed quickly. The Realtor gets her commission and the seller gets his cash. We usually say something like this: "Hi, John, on the offer I just submitted, you will notice that I put the closing date down for next Tuesday. I have cash burning a hole in my pocket and am anxious to start renovating the property. Please let your seller know that I am ready to close as soon as the title company is ready."
5. **Nonrefundable earnest money**. The earnest money deposited with the title company on a typical real estate transaction in the $100,000 range is $1,000. One percent earnest money would be a good rule of thumb for a typical real estate transaction.

Whenever we find a property that we *gotta have* or one we think might receive multiple offers, we drastically increase the amount of earnest money and present it as nonrefundable. The communication would go something like this: "Hi, John, I just e-mailed you my offer on 123 Main Street. On page two of the contract, you will notice the $10,000 *nonrefundable* earnest money. I'm sure you have had many people interested in your listing and wanted to reassure the seller, if they accept my offer, we have a solid deal." Always define the terms of the earnest money as being nonrefundable. It is only nonrefundable if *we* fail to close on the property. The money *is* refundable if the title company cannot issue clear title on the property and close the deal. This one strategy has helped us purchase hundreds of properties because the nonrefundable earnest money gave the seller confidence that he has a solid deal. Always make the earnest money check payable to the title company, *not* the seller.

6. **Pay 100 percent of the closing costs**. Sellers always want to know how much they are going to "walk away with" after they sell their home. When they understand your offer, they are much more likely to sign the contract. Closing costs, title insurance, and commissions all muddy the water for many sellers and make them nervous about signing the offer. The way to alleviate their concerns is to pay 100 percent of their closing costs. This keeps it simple for the seller and gives them the peace of mind they are looking for. The communication would go something like this: "Mitch, I know that you are asking $95,000 for your house. I am willing to pay you $80,000 cash and I will pay for all of your closing costs. In other words, when you show up at the title company to collect the proceeds from the sale, you will walk away with $80,000 minus whatever you owe for property taxes." (If a Realtor is involved, the seller pays the commission.) The reason that we keep property taxes separate is because we often don't know if the seller is current on their taxes. Offering to pay all closing costs gives the seller the certainty they are looking for and will help close many deals.

7. **Pay list price or more**. As we previously mentioned, list price is not always a good indicator of true value. Oftentimes we offer to pay full price or even more. Some savvy Realtors purposely price their properties well below market value to create an auction-type environment. Guess what? It works! Multiple buyers start bidding against one another and the home usually gets sold pretty close to market value. When you know the values in the area, don't be afraid to pay more than asking price if there is still room for a nice profit to be made.
8. **Drafting the perfect email**. To summarize our strategies and illustrate our acquisition philosophy, we are providing you a sample e-mail. Whenever we draft an e-mail to a Realtor, we are really writing it to the seller. Most of the time, the Realtor will just forward our e-mail directly to the seller. If you are working with a Realtor, we would suggest giving them a sample of our e-mail or drafting one yourself and asking them to send it. Remember, your Realtor represents *you*. They have a fiduciary responsibility to help you get the best deal possible. Here is what a typical e-mail from our acquisition team would look like:

Hi, John, attached is my offer on 123 Main Street. This is a *cash* offer with a closing date of next Wednesday. I purchase a lot of homes in the area and feel that my offer represents a very fair offer from a cash investor. The roof looks like it needs replacing and the house needs a ton of updating. The A/C system also looks quite old. My offer price is $74,000. This is the most I am willing to pay. I am willing to buy the house *as is* and do not plan on doing a formal inspection. I am not asking for an option period and there are no contingencies. I am willing to close as soon as the title company has the paperwork ready for us. Please note in the contract, I am willing to put up $10,000 of nonrefundable earnest money and I will even pay for all of the closing costs other than your commission and property taxes. I would appreciate a quick response and hopefully an acceptance of this offer today. I do have my eye on a couple of more homes, but this is my first choice. If your seller does not accept my offer, I need to move quickly on the other properties.

Thanks in advance for contacting your seller right away and getting back to me ASAP.

Erik Saengerhausen

If you master these strategies and take action, you will consistently buy homes under market value and be one step closer to building massive streams of income. Now, let's get down to business and learn how to spend our dollars wisely during the renovation process so that you can deliver a home to the marketplace that will sell lightning quick for top dollar *and* make a nice profit in the process.

ERIK AND MIKE'S BOTTOM LINE:
You really have to stay on top of your target areas and be prepared to move quickly when you find a deal. Having the right Realtor is key. Make sure you develop a very good working relationship and friendship with your Realtor, and if you are not getting the service you expect, find another one.

"Effectiveness in human endeavor calls for the organized budgeting of time. For the average man, the twenty-four hours each day should be divided as follows: eight hours for sleep, eight hours for work, eight hours for recreation and spare time.

"The successful person budgets time, income and expenditures, living within his means. The failure squanders time and income with a contemptuous disregard for their value.

"Tell me how you use your spare time and how you spend your money and I will tell you where and what you will be ten years from now."

—*Napoleon Hill*

6

TURNING A DUCK INTO AN EAGLE

Mr. Juan Madrigal recently moved to San Antonio, Texas, from California with a pocket full of cash ready to invest. Juan had extensive experience in real estate investing in California but was new to the Texas market. Juan had just finished renovating his first home that he planned to flip.

The exterior of the home had a stucco finish and an outstanding paint job. He even built a six-foot stucco wall all around the backyard for added privacy. The inside of the house had gorgeous travertine floors and a massive rock fireplace. The entire home had been completely rewired and had new light fixtures. The kitchen cabinets were custom built and had granite countertops and stainless-steel appliances. The house showed great. Even the windows were new. There was just one problem. There was a huge discrepancy between the price of *his* house and the surrounding homes for sale.

Juan contacted us because he knew we bought and sold homes in the area and wanted to get our opinion of his property. Juan showed us around the house. He was a true craftsman and had extensive experience working on homes. We could tell he was really proud of the job he had done. Juan had been a contractor and investor in California and moved to San Antonio to be closer to his parents. After Juan gave us the tour we asked him how much he was asking for the home. He told us $130,000. He said this was his first

San Antonio rehab and he wanted to make a modest profit and continue to flip homes. Juan told us he had paid $45,000 for the house and spent about $60,000 on the renovation. He thought $130,000 was a very fair price for the home. Juan asked us what we thought about the house. He knew we were investors so we had to shoot straight with him.

We told Juan that the house was beautiful, but unless he was lucky enough to get someone to come along and pay him cash for the home, we did not think that the home would appraise for what he was asking and it would be next to impossible for a buyer to get a loan. The home was only about a thousand square feet. and most of the homes in the area were selling for only about $75 to $80 per square foot. Juan had his home priced at about $130 per square foot! We told Juan that if someone wanted to spend $130K, there are several other areas in the city that would be much more desirable. We suggested that his best strategy to make a profit was to offer owner financing, which he wanted nothing to do with. Juan said that all of his money was tied up and he needed his cash to buy another home to flip. He asked us what we would be willing to pay him for the house. We told Juan that we would pay him $70,000 cash and we close in three days. His face turned about three shades of red and he started laughing.

Fast-forward nine months. Juan called and was ready to make a deal. He told us had he recently taken a job and wanted out of the real estate investment business for good. We sold the house within one week with owner-financing terms and made a nice profit.

Each year about 20 percent of the homes we purchase are from other investors who got in over their heads on a flip project. There is not much room for error on a traditional flip transaction. When flipping a property, you are generally trying to attract a buyer who can qualify for a traditional mortgage so you can cash out. Since the target qualified buyer can purchase *any* home on the market, your property needs to stand out as one of the best if you expect to get top dollar and make a profit.

With seller financing, you are impressing the buyer by the fact that you are offering seller-financing terms, not necessarily with the upgrades and condition of the house. Of course, the home has to be nice, safe, and livable, but it does not have to be renovated to the max. This distinction is huge. Focus on delivering a clean, nice home with *some* upgrades and the seller-financing terms will seal the deal *and* you will get top dollar and make a nice profit.

When we are determining our rehab budget on a property, we focus on three distinct categories of repairs and then estimate the cost for those repairs to determine our budget:

1. Safety issues (must be taken care of)
2. In-your-face Issues (must be taken care of)
3. Over the top (We identify a few things that will make the home really stand out and set it apart from other homes on the market.)

We use the following worksheet to identify the scope of work needed so that we can meet with our contractors and pin down our renovation budget:

Safety Issues:

____$____________________
____$____________________
____$____________________
____$____________________
____$____________________
____$____________________

In-Your-Face Issues:

____$____________________
____$____________________
____$____________________
____$____________________
____$____________________

Over-the-Top Items:

____$____________________
____$____________________
____$____________________
____$____________________
____$____________________

Let's take a look at some examples below of issues that would fit into each category:

SAFETY ISSUES

1. A couple of outlets in the garage look burned and it looks like the outside electrical panel has wires hanging out of it as though it has been tampered with. (Get an estimate from an electrician to address the issues.)
2. We smell gas at a property. (Get an estimate from a plumber to do a pressure test on the gas lines to detect any possible leaks.)
3. Tree branches potentially causing damage. Many homes have trees or tree limbs that could cause significant damage to the house or a neighbor's house. (Get an estimate for trimming or removing the entire tree.)
4. The back patio is missing a corner post and has a lot of rotten wood. It looks like the roof could potentially cave in. (Get an estimate from a carpenter to demo or rebuild the patio.)
5. The swimming pool is unfenced and full of green nasty water. (Get estimates to drain and clean the pool and/or fence the area off for safety.)
6. Smoke alarms and CO_2 detectors are missing. (They need to be installed according to building codes in your area.)

IN-YOUR-FACE ISSUES

In-Your-Face issues are items that absolutely must be done in order to market the home. We would get estimates on all items like these and add it to our renovation budget:

1. The roof looks like it has not been replaced in forty years. There are several shingles missing and obvious signs of rotten roof decking.
2. The carpet is stained and smells. Cleaning will not help. The previous occupant let their dogs live inside the house.
3. The kitchen cabinets have several missing cabinet doors and drawers, and the Formica countertops have several burn marks and cracks and need to be replaced.
4. The tub in the bathroom is clogged and draining very slowly and the toilet tank has a big crack in it.
5. There are five broken windows.
6. There is trash all over the yard and in the garage.
7. There are several light fixtures missing throughout the house.
8. All three bedroom doors have holes that were kicked in and need to be replaced.

OVER-THE-TOP ITEMS

Over-the-top items are the additional renovations we believe will push the home over the top and make it extremely marketable. Making a home marketable can be any combination of improvements to the home that will entice a prospective buyer to purchase the property. Remember, offering seller-financing terms is the *number one* thing that makes your home marketable. This is why it is much easier and more profitable to renovate and sell the home.

Picture a home that has not been updated for twenty years and needs a little bit of everything. Let's assume you already got estimates on the Safety Issues and the In-Your-Face Issues. Here is an example of some of the estimates we would get in order to push the home over the top. Remember, the goal is to present a home that is safe and clean with enough upgrades to motivate a buyer to purchase the property. Here are some examples of things we could do to push a home over the top:

1. Install a brand-new central heating and air-conditioning system: $4,500
2. Update the kitchen with brand-new cabinets and countertops: $5,300

3. Paint the inside and outside of the house: $5,000
4. Install a privacy fence since the neighbor has a barking dog: $2,500
5. Install all new light fixtures, doors, doorknobs, faucets, and windows: $4,000
6. Sand and refinish the wood floors: $2,500

Back in our flipping days, we felt like we had to do *absolutely everything* on this list in order to get a home sold, and therefore it was much harder to squeeze out a profit. With seller financing, we can pick and choose a few items from the list and our homes will still sell for top dollar quickly. Why? Once again, the fact that you are offering seller financing.

Remember the formula for determining the maximum purchase price we learned about in the last chapter? Here it is again:

> ARV (After Repair Value)- [TARGET PROFIT + COST OF REPAIRS] = MAXIMUM PURCHASE PRICE

Unlike flipping properties, when you offer seller financing you have some flexibility on the "cost of repairs" part of the formula. You can do a minimal rehab and still sell your home for top dollar. Are you starting to get the picture? Definitely do *some* updates and improvements, but don't over-rehab it! Take care of Safety Issues and the other In-Your-Face issues and then spend the rest of your money on a few things that will make the home marketable. If you over-rehab the house and renovate it to the max, you will eat up all your profit. It simply is not necessary when you are offering seller financing.

Generally speaking, our philosophy is to spend our money on kitchens and bathrooms. Making the kitchen and bathrooms "pop" has helped us sell hundreds of homes. Things like new doorknobs, light fixtures and faucets can also really give the home an updated look without spending a lot of money.

Flooring is another important subject to discuss. Many older homes have beautiful hardwood floors hiding under several layers of carpet and linoleum. Many rookie investors just slap another layer of cheap carpet or linoleum over the existing layers. Smart investors know that refinished wood floors will help sell the home for top dollar. If you are fortunate enough to have real wood floors, hire someone to remove all of the old layers and then sand and refinish the floors. It is actually relatively inexpensive compared to many other flooring options. Speaking from experience, if the floors "sand out" nicely, meaning they do not have a lot of really bad stains, always go with a "natural" finish. A natural finish means there is no stain involved in the sealing process. The sealant is basically a clear coat of polyurethane. We have seen many rookies go to all of the trouble to refinish the floors only to stain them a very dark color. Dark floors hide the natural beauty of the wood and show all the dirt and dust. We have learned over the years that a much higher percentage of buyers prefer the natural finish over the dark-stained look. We only use a stain when the floors have significant discoloration even after sanding.

Every rehab has a different budget. At the very least, the goal should be to get the home safe and "move-in ready." Move-in ready at a very minimum means that the plumbing and electrical systems are working properly, smoke alarms and CO_2 detectors are installed for safety, and the house is professionally cleaned. There have been many times we have done very minimal rehabs and ended up with an extremely marketable home that sells very quickly for a nice profit.

Homes that need "minimal" rehabs are tougher to buy below market value because you are competing with more buyers. There are many homeowners and landlords who are looking for "good deals," and homes that need only minimal work often get snatched up at a higher price than we are willing to pay. Also, do not underestimate the value that you can bring to a property just by hauling all of the trash out of the yard, trimming overgrown trees, and detail-cleaning. The goal should be to make the place look like grandma lived there. Even if the home is not updated, the fact that the yard looks great and the house has been cleaned goes a long way. Detail-clean *everything*, and don't forget the windows!

CONTRACTORS

Contractors…you can't live with them and you can't live without them. Finding a contractor to do good work is not hard. Finding a good contractor to do good work at a price low enough so that you can still make a profit is another story. The reality of the real estate investment business, especially at the lower-end price points, is that it is extremely competitive. As we mentioned earlier, many people are chasing the same homes that you are and it is challenging to find homes priced under market value. If you plan on squeezing out a profit, you have to get your repairs done at a very reasonable price. Prices from contractors are literally all over the board. We have received bids for an interior paint job that ranged from $1,500 to $6,500. We have had bids from electricians to rewire a home ranging from $3,500 to $12,500 and roof estimates from $3,500 to $8,000! These bids were all on the same house!

Whenever we have received bids from well-known remodeling companies, the prices have been so high that there was no way we could end up making a profit. In many larger companies, there are so many layers of management and overhead that they have to charge higher prices to support their business model and advertising budget. Many homeowners are willing to pay higher prices for the peace of mind that they are going with a reputable company. This is fine for them, but not for us. We are looking for a self-employed guy in a pickup who does most of the work himself and maybe has a helper or two. These are the same guys who a lot of the big companies subcontract to. Our phones are crammed full of contacts for tile guys, painters, plumbers, and electricians. Many of these guys come and go like the wind, so always be proactive in looking for new, quality, affordable contractors.

A couple of years ago, we hired a contractor to rehab a house for us. He had recently started his own business and had previously worked for a large painting company. He had about ten years of experience painting homes. He was just what we were looking for: a hungry entrepreneur with experience! His business card said "Handyman Services" and it listed tile, plumbing, painting, and carpentry work. The plumber we normally used was on vacation, and our tile guy was tied up on a large commercial job. We decided to hire this handyman to do the entire job. We negotiated a price to do all of the painting, tile work, and plumbing since we were adding a second bathroom to the house.

We drove by the house several times the first week. Everything was flowing along smoothly and it looked like the job was going to be done on time and on budget. Toward the end of the project, we stopped in to check on the job. The new bathroom looked great and the paint job was awesome, but the tile countertops and tile floors looked *horrible*! More than eight-hundred square feet of tile had been laid, and the "lines" were off big time. He had also made an executive decision and used black grout with our beige tile! It looked like an ugly crooked checkerboard! The tile countertops were also horrendous. He had left a half-inch tile strip along the back edge of the counter, and the surface was not smooth at all. We tried to keep our cool and asked him, "What the hell happened?" He said that he had been around people laying tile for years, but we were only his second tile job! Ugh…

We ended up having to beg our regular tile guy to come in on a weekend and blow out the entire job and redo it. The new tile job got done and we finally got the home sold. About two days after the new owner moved into the house, he called us because he said the toilet in his brand-new bathroom kept "gurgling." We sent our plumber over to the house to try to snake out the line. He tried several times, but the problem persisted. He finally removed the toilet and discovered that the painter-turned-"handyman" had used a drain pipe TOO SMALL for a toilet! The plumber had to jackhammer into the slab to change the pipe! The moral of the story is to let your plumber do the plumbing, let the tile guy lay tile, and let the painter paint. Trust us on this one: stick with specialists, not the handyman.

When you are new to the real estate investing game, it can be challenging trying to figure out what a fair price is for getting a job done. When you are first getting started, we would suggest getting several bids for all aspects of your renovation so you can get a good idea what contractors are charging in your area. While vacationing in Lake Tahoe a while back, we came across a contractor who was about to paint the interior of the condo next door to the one we were staying in. We told him we were in the real estate business in Texas and asked what he was getting paid to paint the interior of the condo. He said he charged the seller $6,000. In San Antonio, we could have gotten the same condo painted for about $2,000. This is why we did not spend a bunch of time in this chapter telling you what you should pay for certain aspects of the renovation process. Labor prices vary greatly depending on what part of the country you are in. The goal of this chapter is to share our philosophy on renovating houses and to drive home the point to *not* over-rehab a house and to focus on the lower end of the market to make sure the monthly payments are consistent with rents in the area.

It won't take you long to get a handle on what is considered a fair and reasonable price for a job in your area. Once you do, we suggest you do the following: meet a contractor at your house and instead of asking him how much he would do the job for, tell him what you are willing to pay. We usually say something like this:

"Hi, John, thanks for meeting us at the house. We are investors and our goal is to fix up this house as professionally and affordably as we can. We seller finance all of our homes to hardworking families that cannot get traditional bank financing. We have fixed up lots of homes over the years and always try to be fair with the contractors we work with. On this house, we are looking for a painter to paint the inside of the house, including the kitchen cabinets and are willing to pay $2,500. That is all we have in the budget for painting. Can you do the job for $2,500?"

If you know that is a fair price, stand your ground and you will find someone to jump on the job. We prefer this approach instead of negotiating back and forth with the contractor. We like "one simple price," as many of the car dealers say. Always make sure there is clear communication regarding who is paying for the materials. Is the $2,500 price just for labor or does it include the paint? Also, be prepared for contractors hitting you up for extra money after they agree on a price to do a job. They will say things like, "I needed to put two coats on the walls because the paint would not cover" or "there were a lot more cracks in the walls than I originally thought." Try to nip these things in the bud up front. Let the contractor know that you are working with a fixed budget and don't want any surprises, and if this job goes well, you will call him again.

One time, we had several rehabs going on and we needed someone to do a quick exterior paint job. All of our main contractors were tied up, so we started thumbing through our wallets looking for a business card from a contractor who had stopped into our office recently looking for work. Sure enough, we found it! We called "Frank" and asked him to meet us at the house to discuss the job. He immediately let us know he really needed the work and would do this job for us for $600. He said he wanted to do it at a really good price so we could see the quality of his work and would hire him again on future projects. We were blown away, and our greedy juices started flowing. We would normally pay about $1,200 to $1,500 for the same job. Frank did a really good job! We paid him the $600 plus materials and moved him to the front of the line on our contractor list.

The next job Frank did was an interior paint job. He said he could paint the entire inside for $1,000. Again, we were blown away and licking our chops on the nice profit we were going to end up with. He had three guys blowing and going, and even his wife was there helping. The job got knocked out lightning fast and Frank was ready for more. Frank told me he had been a contractor in California and he was trying to get established here in Texas.

He said that he had run multiple crews and he would really appreciate the opportunity to do more and more of our jobs. His prices were amazing! Every job we gave to Frank was about 50 percent off what we had been paying and the quality was decent.

We finally opened up the floodgates and gave Frank three major rehab projects at one time. He had earned our trust. Frank asked for $3,000 on each house to start getting all the materials together for his crews. That was a reasonable request so we cut him a check for $9,000. The next day we ran by to check on one of the projects and nobody was there. We assumed all the workers must have been at one of the other projects so we went by the other two houses. No workers. We called Frank and the call went straight to voicemail. We spent the next couple of weeks trying to track him down and even went by his house multiple times.

Frank disappeared on us and we never saw him again. It was "only" $9,000, but we learned a valuable lesson: just give a contractor one job at a time and do not advance him too much money. As the saying goes, "If it seems too good to be true, it probably is."

We have just a few more comments about rehabbing before we teach you how to sell a house in less than thirty days without a Realtor. If the renovation project calls for a permit from your local governmental authority, go ahead and pay the fee and do the proper paperwork. If you get caught doing work without a permit, city officials can fine you and make your life miserable. Just follow the rules. You will sleep better at night knowing you don't have to be looking over your shoulder at the job site.

We have also learned that vacant homes are often the target of vandalism. Keep a light on in the house while it is being worked on and ask your neighbors to keep an eye on the property for you. Oftentimes we ask a neighbor to park one of their cars in our driveway while the home is being rehabbed.

You would be surprised at how willing and cooperative neighbors are in this regard. They love to protect their turf and help us protect ours.

We have learned the hard way that there are a lot of thieves in the world. We cannot tell you how many stoves, refrigerators, and air conditioners have been stolen from our homes. Probably enough to fill the showroom at Lowe's! We have reached the point where we never install appliances until after the home closes, and oftentimes we actually pay an air conditioning guy to remove and store the outside A/C condensing unit until the house sells. When a home has a "For Sale" sign in the yard and is vacant, it is an invitation to thieves to come and help themselves.

You are one step closer to creating a beautiful stream of income! You found a great deal, stuck to your budget, and rehabbed the house. Now what? Find a buyer with good character with some money in his pocket!

ERIK AND MIKE'S BOTTOM LINE:
Don't over-rehab your houses. Give a contractor only one job at a time. Make sure the guy you are paying is on the job 99 percent of the time. You don't want the contractor to send "his guys" to do your job. You want him to be one of the guys who is always there.

"Render more and better service than that for which you are paid, and sooner or later you will receive compound interest on compound interest from your investment. For it is inevitable that every seed of every useful service you sow will multiply itself and come back to you in overwhelming abundance.

"Put your mind to work. Assess your ability and energy. Who could use your help? How can you help? It doesn't take money...all it takes is ingenuity and a strong desire to be of genuine service. Helping others to solve their problems will help you to solve your own.

"The most successful people are those who serve the greatest number of people."

—*Napoleon Hill*

7

A BUTT FOR EVERY SEAT

You have successfully rehabbed the property and now it is time to market and sell it. What do you do? How do you market it? How long will it take to sell? How do you know what price to list it at? These questions and more will be answered in this chapter.

There are several critical steps involved in selling your property that if neglected, can leave a substantial chunk of change on the table. We will show you how to sell any house in thirty days for your full asking price 95 percent of the time.

Selling a house is one of the most underrated aspects of real estate investing. Most investors will spend thousands on education, learning how to find and rehab houses, but never give one thought or spend one dime to learn how to properly sell them. That's like buying a brand-new car but not knowing how to drive it! It doesn't make any sense. In this chapter we will teach you how to market a house correctly so you can find the right person to buy it and do so quickly! Remember, there is a butt for every seat and it's your job to find it!

The home you rehabbed has to be marketed and sold. Does that make you nervous? It should. You will find out very quickly whether you bought the house for the right price and whether your rehab stayed within budget. Did you do the right renovations to push it "over the top" and take care of the safety issues? Are you terrified what an inspector might find that could mess up your deal? Are you able to price the house at or below market value and still make a nice profit, or do you have to overprice it and pray to the "flip gods" that the house will sell? As the old saying goes, "You make money when you buy! But you don't realize it until you sell!"

Let's assume you bought the house "right," did a fantastic rehab job, and even came in under budget. Now what? It's now time to come up with a sales price and marketing plan.

When you are new to the business, it is wise to ask a Realtor to give you a comparative market analysis (CMA) on your house. This is very difficult to do if you do not have access to the MLS system, so befriending a Realtor is a good idea. A CMA will give you an idea of what other houses in your neighborhood are selling for and what yours "should" sell for. It will also let you know the average number of days a home is usually on the market, which is very important. You should price your property *at or slightly below market value* to sell quickly, *not above market value*!

Let's say you are going to sell a home in the $150,000 range and the Realtor tells you the average home in the neighborhood in that price range is selling in an average of 180 days. If this is the case, you might consider listing your home slightly under market value so it will sell more quickly. The money you save by potentially selling it in thirty or sixty days versus 180 days is huge. You can realize a profit and go find another property and do it again.

We usually like to look only at homes that have sold in the past six months when preparing a comparative market analysis. If you are looking at comps (comparable sales) from twelve months or older, the market may have changed for the better or worse and you might end up selling the home too cheaply, or, even worse, overpricing it and losing time, which equals money and eventually loss of profit.

We consistently turn our properties in about one hundred and twenty days from start to finish and we have done it hundreds and hundreds of times. If we raised our prices, our houses would sit on the market longer and we would realize a yearly net profit significantly lower than we do taking a smaller profit and "turning our money" every four months. We like to say we take the "Costco" approach to selling houses. How fast can we buy, rehab, and sell, get our capital back, make a decent profit, and do it again. Price it right, sell it fast, make your money, and move on to the next one. Don't try to hit a home run on every deal. If you swing and miss, it could cost you a lot of money!

OVERPRICED LISTINGS

Story from Erik: *I see it all the time. I will be looking though the MLS for properties to buy and I come across a listing owned by an investor who has been trying to sell his home for a very, very long time. Why hasn't it sold yet? I am always curious.*

Here is one I recently came across:

three-bedroom, two bath
1,400 square feet
0.25-acre lot in a great subdivision
Price: $119,900

The agent's remarks: "This home has been rehabbed from top to bottom. New granite countertops, tile floors, new fixtures, new central A/C! Bring your client today! This home won't last long!"

Wow! I think to myself as I am scrolling through the pictures of the house. What a great-looking property! I then scroll down to "Days on Market." Three hundred forty-two days on the market! Almost a YEAR! What happened to "This home won't last long"?

It seems to be priced right…

I'm intrigued about why this home did not sell quickly, so I dig deeper. I look at the history of the property listing and see that the Realtor reduced the price more than fifteen times! The initial list price was $149,900, which was way overpriced for the neighborhood. They dropped the price only $2,000 every time and did so fifteen different times over the course of almost a year and it still has not sold. Why? What did they do wrong?

It could be a few things:

1. **They did not do a CMA and just listed it for what they "hoped" it would sell for**. This happens all the time! Or they will list it for how much profit they want to make instead of what the house is actually worth.
2. **They over-rehabbed the home and needed to sell high just to break even.** We see this all the time too. This is probably the number one reason many investor flip houses are overpriced. This will backfire on you every time and in the end cost you even more money. It's like doubling down on a bad bet. If you spent too much money on your rehab, take your loses early and move on to the next deal.
3. **Their Realtor told them it was worth $149,000.** I doubt this is the case, but it would not surprise me if the Realtor suggested a much lower list price and the seller totally dismissed the suggestions and the data on the CMA. There are so many Realtors trying to get listings, many of them will agree to list something high just to get their name out into the marketplace. They probably know darn well that the home will never sell for the listed amount, but quite frankly, they don't care. The client is using them and they are using their client. In the end, they both end up losing. The client doesn't get the house sold, and the Realtor gets a bad reputation for overpricing his or her listings.

So why has the property not sold if it is now priced at the correct value?

Because it's gotten a bad rap!

Most Realtors look at days on market and the pricing history prior to deciding whether or not they should show a home to their client. Many days on the market with multiple price changes throws up a red flag. They start to think something is wrong with the house and that's why it has been on the market for so long and had the multiple price drops. Realtors often relay this information to their buyer, who now thinks something is wrong with the house or even worse, they never even let their buyer know about the house because they don't want to waste their time. The vicious downward spiral of the price reductions and no offers begins, and it is a *long* way down to the bottom!

I went back and researched the house as I am writing this story, and the house did end up selling, but *only* for $109,900. It was on the market for 376 days! Ouch!

If the seller and Realtor had priced it at $119,900 right out of the gate, the seller could have sold the house, bought another one, and probably sold that one too. Instead, he swung for the fences and it cost him and his money an entire year of sitting on the sidelines.

YOU HOLD THE GOLD

One very important theme we have been preaching throughout this book is that when you seller finance a property, you "Hold the Gold." You should be able to get top dollar without having to negotiate. Typically we do not negotiate with Realtors or buyers on price or terms. We lay out our terms and they either accept them or move on. Most of the time they accept them. Every now and again if the buyer is very strong and has a very large down payment (20 percent or more) we will negotiate a little on interest but almost never on price. *Negotiating the interest rate is better than reducing the price because lowering the price cuts into your profit. We have never had a problem selling a real estate note with a large down payment, regardless of it having a lower-than-normal interest rate.* By the way, a "low" interest rate in our world would be 9 or 10 percent. In other words, note buyers will generally be willing to accept a lower yield on a note if there is a sizable down payment.

INSPECTORS

Once you have a home under contract, the buyer might want to get the home inspected. We encourage all of our buyers to have the home inspected but let them know up front that we will not make any repairs and that our houses are sold as is. *Obviously, there are some exceptions to this rule. If the inspector discovers something that will endanger the lives of the people living in the home, we will address it, but that would be about it.* All other minor items we will not address. When you sell traditional flips, you will be on the hook for almost all items listed on the inspection report because the buyer has his own financing and will probably go buy another home if you don't step up and fix all of the issues. When you offer seller financing, you call the shots!

An inspection report can be a great bargaining tool when buying a house and a profit killer when selling one! The inspector's job is to find problems associated with the house, and, trust me, they will! We have sold brand-new houses, and we have sold old rundown houses, and the inspector has found something wrong with both of them. Inspection issues on a brand-new house? Can you believe that? Believe it! Imagine what they might find on a home that is fifty or sixty years old!

Inspectors have to disclose every minor or major problem they come across. They do so because they want the buyer to know exactly what they are purchasing and they don't want to get sued for not finding a problem that arises after the sale. Inspectors look for electrical and plumbing issues, heating and A/C issues and also roof and foundation concerns. What do you think will happen if a buyer moves in and discovers the house he just purchased has a significant foundation problem that the inspector failed to recognize? We live in a very litigious world and would not be surprised if the buyer called a lawyer. What sucks about many inspectors is that they have gotten so paranoid about missing something on an inspection report and getting sued that they cover their butts by putting down statements like this on their report: "I recommend that you consult with an engineer and foundation company to further assess your property," or "I recommend that you hire a professional roofer to assess your roof," or "I recommend that you hire an electrician, A/C guy and plumber." This just confuses the buyer and in our opinion renders the inspector just about useless. If he is just going to recommend getting a professional to take a look at every part of the home, why did he get hired?

Story from Erik: *I recently sold a townhouse just outside of San Antonio and it was literally remodeled from top to bottom. Everything was new! The guy we bought it from took it down to the studs and planned on totally renovating the unit. He ran out of money about 90 percent from completion and called us. He needed money and wanted cash fast. I offered him $60,000 cash and he accepted it even though he said he had almost $70,000 invested. It was located in an area that we don't normally buy in and it was a townhouse, so I decided to do a traditional flip instead of offering seller financing. I don't really like doing traditional flips, but this one just looked too easy to pass up.*

You're probably wondering why someone would lose money on a house. There are a number of reasons. Here are some of the most common ones I see:

1. *Flipping a house looked easy on TV and they got in over their head.*
2. *Health problems.*
3. *Family emergency and they need cash NOW.*
4. *Divorce*
5. *Job relocation*

We finished the rehab in less than a week, listed it at $99K, and within five days we had a cash buyer offer us $95K with a ten-day option period and it was scheduled to close in fourteen days. We accepted the offer. The potential buyer had an inspection scheduled on the second day of the ten-day option period and we did not hear back from them for several days. We foolishly assumed that since this *house was completely redone from top to bottom and we had not heard from the buyer that we were on track to a smooth $25K profit in less than thirty days. Never happens! Of course the inspector found several things wrong with the house. There were signs of "previous" termite infestation and damage in the garage and the buyer wanted it treated and a letter stating there were no termites, even though the Wood Destroying Insect Report from the inspector said there were no "active" termites. They also wanted a tree hanging over the garage completely removed "in case it fell" and they wanted the roof checked by a licensed roofer, and, of course, the roofer recommended the roof needed to be replaced real soon. The end of the story is that our profit went from $25K to $15K.*

This particular deal was on one of the few traditional flips we do each year. Ninety-five percent of our transactions are seller-finance deals, but every now and then we have a deal come along that looks like "easy flip money" and we pull the trigger. In hindsight, we could have offered seller financing on this property and probably made a better profit. We stuck with the flip game plan on the deal because it was a townhome in an area we don't normally focus on buying in and most of our note buyers don't buy townhome notes.

When you offer seller financing, you are bringing so much value to the buyer they will tend to go forward with the home purchase and deal with the inspection issues on their own.

SELL YOUR HOUSE IN THIRTY DAYS OR LESS

Let's talk about marketing and how to make money! We do that when we sell the house quickly to the right buyer and for top dollar. Marketing your house can be defined as the way in which you present your property to the public that will entice a buyer to purchase it. Our goal is to market the home WITHOUT a Realtor and WITHOUT spending a lot of money. By eliminating a real estate commission and all of the headaches that go along with working with Realtors, you will end up making more profit. Realtors are wired to try to negotiate on price and interest rates and also are programmed to ask for a bunch of inspection issues to be taken care of. If you follow our marketing strategies, you will not have to deal with Realtors or negotiate on your price and terms. In our real estate course, we will teach you how to find a good real estate attorney who can provide all of the necessary documents needed to close a transaction for a fraction of the cost compared to paying a real estate commission.

Many investors think that slapping a sign up in the front yard is all you need. That is the laziest thing you can do. How hard was that? How much time did it take you to drive to the house, get out of your car, and stomp on a metal sign until it would stand up straight. Heck, we have seen some that couldn't even make it that far! They half-a** try to stick it in the ground, but the ground is too hard so they give up and lean it against a tree! Maybe it was really HOT or COLD that day or *American Idol* was coming on TV soon and they had to hurry to get home.

So, how do you market a home with seller-financing terms AND sell it quickly?

Cleaning and Staging

You should have the house cleaned from top to bottom, including the windows, by a professional cleaning company. Don't underestimate the marketing power of a CLEAN home. We have found that buyers love walking into a clean house. Be sure to get all of the hard-to-reach places, too. Clean the tops of the cabinets, ceiling-fan blades, closets, and even wipe down the water heater. Women notice these things! The same thing goes for the yard. Trim any tree branches and bushes that are overgrown and too close to the house. Mow, rake, and edge the yard until you have the best-looking lawn on the block. The positive psychological effect that a clean house and a manicured lawn have on a buyer is huge. Even if the house is extremely outdated and in need of repair, the price someone will pay for a clean house with a manicured yard is significantly higher than one that is filthy and overgrown.

Staging a home is another great way to make the home feel more warm and inviting. Staging can be a very effective and inexpensive way to add some "flare" to your property. You can warm up a house by doing some minimal staging for less than $500, and once the property sells, just move your staging supplies to the next one. The goal is to make the property feel more like a HOME, not just a HOUSE. In a typical home, we would do the following:

1. Put a new "Welcome Mat" by the front door.
2. Put a few artificial plants in pots on the front porch to add some color and warmth to the exterior of the home.
3. Hang some towels and wash cloths in the bathrooms and add a nice shower curtain.
4. Place some nice inexpensive rugs in various parts of the home to give it some warmth and color.
5. Place some canisters on the kitchen counter. The kind you would store flour and sugar in.
6. Place some flowers in a vase and have them on the kitchen counter.
7. If there is a fireplace, place a few decorative items on the mantel.
8. Install a couple of plug-in air fresheners.

Do you get the picture? All of these ideas bring some warmth and color to the home. It really does not take much to help make a good first impression for the buyer. The buying process is emotionally driven. Deliver a clean, warm home to the marketplace and you will get top dollar and sell it quickly every time.

When you are first getting started, go into a Good Will store and see what you can find to stage your first house. If you strike out there, just go to Walmart and Hobby Lobby and you will be ready to rock.

Who Is Your Buyer?

You must understand the different demographics involved in each neighborhood in which you are selling. You must know who your customer is in order to market to them properly.

Ours is typically a Hispanic-based neighborhood with ages ranging from thirty-five to sixty-five. Most have family in the near vicinity.

Two out of every five people who buy a home from us have a relative who lives in the immediate area.

Most of our buyers speak Spanish. Because of that, almost all of our advertising is in English and Spanish. Also, many of our targeted buyers read the local neighborhood Spanish publications. Because we understand who our customers are, we know that in order to get in front of our potential buyer we need to be advertising in the right places and to the right people.

You really have to understand *who your clients are* in order to properly and effectively market to them. You wouldn't advertise on your local rock-and-roll radio station if you were marketing a retirement home, would you? First, understand who you are marketing to, and second, understand what they do on a daily basis. What are they reading? What radio station do they listen to? Are they on Facebook? Where do they work? What do they do on the weekends? Do they watch sports or have kids who play sports? Once you have figured out who your target market is, then you will be able to target your marketing to appeal to those potential home buyers.

Below are some methods we use on every house we sell. By using these marketing methods, along with knowing who our customers are, we are able to sell 95 percent of our houses in thirty days or less.

10-10-20 Marketing

The 10-10-20 is a marketing strategy we adopted somewhere along the way. It works! Make a simple flyer about the house you are selling and put it on the door of the ten houses on the right and ten houses on the left of your house as well as the twenty houses across the street. This will get the word out to your neighbors that your home is for sale.

Most people like to have someone they know and like living next to them. The biggest fear a neighbor has is some deadbeat moving next to them and ruining the neighborhood. They now have a vested interest in finding you a potential buyer for your house. We sell many houses to friends and family members of our neighbors. This method is very easy and will take less than thirty minutes. Keep the flyer simple with a picture of the house with all the details: beds, baths, square footage, price, and so on.

Craigslist

You should be listing all your houses for sale on Craigslist. It's *free* and easy to do. You will need to repost every couple of days to keep your listing near the top. If you are close to other cities, advertise in those areas as well. If your city gets a lot of "transfers" from other states, then advertise on their Craigslist pages as well. There is a lot of competition on Craigslist, but if you are religious about posting your homes for sale it can be very lucrative. Make it a habit to post daily, and you should get some great responses.

Postlets

Postlets.com is a great way to create a very professional flyer that you can print, e-mail or blast out into the Internet. (Use this flyer for your 10-10-20 marketing mentioned above.) You can also post your Postlet into Craigslist for a more professional ad.

Marketing is basically answering this question: *How can I stand out among my competitors and attract people who would benefit from my product?* Postlets will help you stand out among your competitors on Craigslist as well as the multitude of other sites they post to. Here is a list of the sites that Postlets currently posts your advertisement to:

- Zillow
- AOL Real Estate
- RentBits

- Walkscore
- RentJungle
- Rentenna
- Zumper
- MapLiv
- RentMatch
- HotPads
- FrontDoor
- Trulia
- LiveLovely
- Enormo
- Oodle
- Military.com
- *New York Post*
- Facebook
- Yahoo!
- MSN Real Estate
- BackPage.com
- ByOwnerMLS
- Vast
- Trovit
- Geebo
- Yakaz
- MyNewPlace

As you can see, it would be foolish to not advertise on Postlets. Plus, it's *free*!

Facebook

Facebook can be a great way to generate interest in your properties if you understand how and where to advertise. You can "boost" a post for as little as $10 and reach thousands of people who are not your "friends." We have gotten very good results from this marketing and generally do it twice a month. You will need to create a "page" just for your investment company. There are entire books written specifically on Facebook marketing. We would highly recommend you buy one and study it.

One other Facebook tip: Whenever you sell a house, offer the buyers a $25 gift card if they will post on their Facebook page that they just bought a house from you with your web address and/or "tag" you in it. This will create a link on the post to your website and it will be viewed by hundreds of your clients' friends and families.

According to statista.com, the average number of friends people have on Facebook per age group is as follows:

Age		Friends
18–24	=	649
25–34	=	360
35–44	=	277
45–54	=	220
55–64	=	129

If you sell four houses a month and every one of them posts a link on their Facebook page about you and your company, then you are indirectly marketing to more than 1,200 people a month for only $100 ($25 gift card x four people)! The good thing about marketing like this is that it is a referral-based marketing technique. One of their friends is recommending you rather than just a generic add that pops up in their face. Referrals tend to have a much higher conversion rate than generic advertising.

Open House

Hold an open house the first two weekends the house hits the market. There are a couple of reasons why you would want to do this. It will help you understand who the buyers are in that neighborhood. It will also provide you with a list of people looking for houses who may not like the one you are selling but could be potential buyers in the future.

If you have multiple houses, you can direct them to another house if they don't like the one you are at. Build a buyers list and hold on to it. Get as much information as you can from the future homebuyers who show up at your open houses. This will be valuable information down the road. We have amassed a huge buyers list from all the marketing techniques we are giving you, and six out of ten homes for sale already have a buyer lined up for it before it hits the market. Here are some tips for your open house:

1. Bake something. People love the smell of cookies baking in the oven, as it will remind them of home. If you don't want to bake, have some bottled water and some cookies or candy for people to snack on.
2. If the weather permits, open the windows and let the fresh air in.
3. Apps. There are apps you can post your open house on. This will boost your attendance! Realtor.com offers an app that will post open houses.
4. Put up some signs: Put up four or five signs near the busiest streets closest to your home. Keep it simple: OPEN HOUSE and the address.
5. Invite the neighbors. Recruit them to help you sell your house. No one wants a bad neighbor, and most will do whatever they can to ensure a good neighbor moves in even if that means helping you find a buyer. We have sold dozens of houses to referrals from one of the neighbors.
6. Balloons: Get a bunch of balloons and attach them to the sign in the front yard. This will draw attention to your property when people drive by, and, I assure you, most of the nosy neighbors will be sure to stop by.

"We must all suffer one of two things: the pain of discipline or the pain of regret or disappointment."

—**Jim Rohn**

Bandit Signs

As we previously discussed in Chapter 4, bandit signs are a cheap and easy way to market. In Chapter 4 we suggested using bandit signs to find properties to *buy*. Now we are talking about using bandit signs to help *sell* your properties. We are often selling multiple houses in the same areas so we tend to do a "blanket" marketing technique. Our strategy is to keep the signs very generic. The signs usually just read: "2 BEDS 1 BATH OWNER FINANCE" OR "3 BEDS 1 BATH OWNER FINANCE."

We intentionally leave out the address. When people call, we have a better chance to direct them to a certain house depending on their wants and needs. If you have only one house, go ahead and put the address on the sign. You should put about ten to fifteen signs within a one-mile radius of your house. We like to put a big arrow on the corner of the busiest streets pointing toward the property. Many people are driving too fast to read the entire sign, but if they see "SELLER FINANCING 3/1" with a huge arrow pointing to the left, they will more than likely turn at the sign and try to find the house.

We like to use yellow or white coroplast and write with big, black permanent Sharpie markers. You can buy coroplast online in bulk four-by-eight sheets then cut them to the size we want with a razor. It will save you hundreds of dollars if you are putting out a lot of signs a month, as we are. If you want your phone to ring, then this is the easiest and most cost-effective way. We call it "pounding the street" or "blasting signs." We sell 75 percent of our houses with this method.

As mentioned in Chapter 4, be sure to check the local rules for signage in your area. Putting up signs is a bit of a cat-and-mouse game. We have found that we do not have any issues with code compliance folks if we have our signs spread out over a wide area. Some cities offer affordable sign permits, which allow you to keep the signs up for a specified time each day. Bandit signs work great, but if you live in a city where they are really tough on signs, focus on some other strategies. With social media, Craigslist, and other electronic forms of advertising, it is not too hard to get the word out about your property.

Website

If you start doing a lot of transactions, creating a website to list your homes for sale is a great way to attract buyers. It should be very simple and have a mobile version too. Most people are using cellphones or tablets to view the Internet, and you want to make sure your website is viewable. Be sure to have lots of pictures and a good description of each house. Pictures are very important to someone looking online for houses. Take as many pictures as you can and make sure they are high quality. *Do not use your cellphone!* Even though picture quality is improving, don't do it. Go buy a good camera; it will pay for itself quickly. Take pictures of bathrooms, the kitchen, the front of the house, back of the house, bedrooms, living rooms, and any other positives that may attract a buyer, such as a huge backyard or swimming pool.

As you grow your business, you can hire an SEO (search engine optimization) company to get your website near the top of search engines or pay for online advertising with companies like Google AdWords. This will get your ranking higher and allow people searching for homes in your area to find you. There are many books that can show you how to "organically" raise your search engine ranking. We are not experts in this area but know your success has a lot to do with linking everything together. Have a Facebook, Twitter, Instagram, and LinkedIn account, and link all of your accounts. This will help your credibility and your Google rankings. You can also post videos of your home on YouTube and write a blog. The more information you have, the better Google and other search engines will like you. Technology is changing quickly. Be sure to keep up with the latest online marketing opportunities and strategies. Especially the ones that are *free*!

IT WON'T SELL...NOW WHAT?

When you offer seller financing, most of the time you will find a buyer within the first thirty days because the demand is so high. So, let's say your house has been on the market for ninety days and no one has made you an offer. Now what do you do?

First, start with the basics. Get the home detail-cleaned *again* and make sure the lawn looks impeccable. Then check your signs and all of your other forms of advertising. Make sure your signs are up and visible. Is there a sign in the front yard? Can you read the phone numbers? Oftentimes, investors make the big mistake of making sure the home looks great when it first hits the market. Then they get lazy and let the lawn go and don't keep the house spit-shined and keep signs up. You want every buyer to feel like the house just got cleaned today!

We then suggest you take a good look at your list price again and have your Realtor pull the most recent comps in the area to make sure you are not priced too high. Assuming you have the home priced correctly, we suggest you give it another thirty days or so. If you still cannot find a buyer, you may consider accepting a slightly lower down payment than you have been offering. In the following chapter on character underwriting, we teach you how to pick out the *right* buyer and get a substantial down payment from the buyer. Accepting a lower down payment than normal is an option, but it also makes the note less attractive to note buyers.

About one time out of fifty, we end up with a home that just won't sell for some reason. Remember, time IS money. If we are sitting on a home for six months, we usually lower our sales price big time and just break even or make a very small profit on the deal. Sometimes it is just better to get your toys back and go play somewhere else. It does not happen often, but that is actually another really great thing about this business model. If things go "wrong" for some reason and the house will not sell, if you followed the steps taught in this book, you should easily be able to get your initial investment back. Hey, making a profit forty-nine out of fifty times are odds we can live with!

Remember, there *is* a butt for every seat, and if you follow the marketing strategies in this chapter, you will have plenty of butts to choose from. The next chapter will teach you how to choose the *right* buyer with a pocket full of money.

ERIK AND MIKE'S BOTTOM LINE:
Price the house at market value, clean the heck out of everything, and make sure your lawn looks great. Signs are the most effective way to market that we have found.

"Don't wish it was easier; wish you were better. Don't wish for fewer problems; wish for more skills. Don't wish for less challenge; wish for more wisdom."

—Jim Rohn

8

CHARACTER UNDERWRITING

Several years ago, three good friends were driving down a country road in west Texas when all of a sudden a tornado came along, picked their car, and tossed it upside down on the highway. All three of the men were killed. Fortunately, they were all believers, and when they "awoke," they found themselves standing in line to get into Heaven. When the three friends finally got to the Pearly Gates, Saint Peter was there checking people in. One of the passengers, Joe, was next in line. Saint Peter said "Joe, Heaven is a very large place, and you are going to need transportation to get around. I have just one question for you that you must answer honestly to be able to enter Heaven and be issued your transportation. The question is this: Have you ever been unfaithful to your wife? Joe smiled and puffed out his chest and said never! Saint Peter said, "Come on in, Joe!" and tossed Joe the keys to a brand-new red Mercedes convertible.

Next up was his friend John. Saint Peter asked John the same question. "John, have you ever been unfaithful to your wife?" John squirmed a little bit and then slowly held up one finger. Saint Peter paused a moment and then said, "Come on in" and tossed John the keys to a 2007 Chevy pickup. Now it was Frank's turn. Saint Peter turned to Frank and said, "Frank, in order to enter Heaven, you must honestly answer the following question: "Have you ever been unfaithful to your wife?" Frank looked away and sheepishly held up four fingers. Saint Peter glared at him for what seemed to be an eternity and said, "Welcome, Frank." He then tossed him the keys to a 1972 Ford Pinto.

The three friends were relieved to all get into Heaven and decided to drive around for a while to check things out. A couple of hours later, they all met at a roadside park. Joe and John both jumped out of their vehicles and were super-excited about what they had seen. Joe said, "Isn't this place amazing?" Frank remained in his vehicle and appeared to be sad and moping. He finally started to slowly open up his door. His face looked weary and his shoulders were slumped. Joe ran up to Frank and said, "Come on, Frank, what's the matter? Are you bummed out about having to drive that old Pinto? Frank said, "No...no...no...I don't have a problem with my car. It's my wife! I just saw her a few minutes ago. She's on roller skates!"

Character matters. Jim Rohn used to say, "Time either promotes you or it exposes you." The goal with character underwriting is to take enough time during the underwriting process to either promote or expose the client. What separates the men from the boys in the seller-finance business model is the commitment to character underwriting. The *men* recognize that offering seller financing means being "married" to a client for a very long time. The *men* also must have the patience to find the "right buyer" *and* have the huevos to *reject* an applicant if they don't feel confident they are dealing with someone of good character. The *boys* take the first warm body that can scrape up $2,000 and "sell" them the house. Selling a home with only $2,000 down is nothing more than a glorified rental. The buyer does not have enough skin in the game.

Before we go into more detail about character underwriting, let's dial in our philosophy and begin with the end in mind. The goal is to create passive streams of income that will flow for years to come. Whether you plan to hold your notes or sell your notes to investors, everyone wants the same thing: mailbox money that shows up month after month and year after year. If too many of your notes have payment problems, investors will quit buying your notes and bankers will quit lending you money. Not to mention the number of headaches and legal expenses that you will incur.

This chapter is focused on character underwriting, but, let's face it, someone with stellar character and no job or money does you no good. We have learned from doing hundreds of transactions that getting the buyer to bring at least 10 percent of the purchase price to closing significantly increases the odds of creating a headache-free stream of income. We can tell you story after story about people who looked at one of our homes and said, "I don't have 10 percent down" and then they call us back a week later with the *cash.* People have a way of coming up with the money. They sell a second vehicle, get a gift from grandma, or let go of some of their "mattress money." Once you get a buyer to commit to a solid 10 percent down, you have gone a long way toward creating a solid and marketable real estate note.

Early on in our seller-finance career, we met with a very successful real estate investor to discuss our business plan. We told him we planned on getting 10 percent down on all of the homes that we sold. He said, "You will *never* get it! These people live paycheck to paycheck. There is no way they can come up with $10,000!" He said he had sold hundreds of homes in the exact same neighborhoods we were targeting, and in fifteen years he had rarely been able to get more than $2,500 from *anyone.* He said we were wasting our time and making a big mistake. His belief system was this: *none of the people who are going to buy my houses have any money for a down payment.* Guess what? That is what he believed and that is what materialized for fifteen years! Our belief is this: *people will find a way to come up with 10 percent down.* Guess what? That is what we believe and it materializes over and over again. Hundreds and hundreds of times! Whatever the mind can conceive and believe, it can achieve. Choose your beliefs carefully and stick to a minimum of 10 percent down!

The number one mistake rookie investors make is selling the house to the first warm body that comes along with a little cash in his pocket. Selling the homes is actually the *easiest* part of the entire process of creating real estate notes. It is much harder to find a property under market value, stay within your budget on the rehab, and find note buyers. When you offer seller-financing terms, sit back and wait for the right buyer who is willing to put at least 10 percent down. The vast majority of the prospective buyers who will respond to a seller-financing advertisement could not qualify for a traditional mortgage. If you happen to come across a buyer who could qualify for a traditional mortgage, the ethical thing to do is to refer them to a traditional mortgage broker so they can get a lower interest rate and better terms.

If you follow our marketing strategies, you will often find yourself in a multiple offer situation. You will have multiple buyers wanting to purchase your home. There is a huge demand for seller financing, and many of the buyers who have been rejected by the big banks will be beating down your door for a financing opportunity. When you receive multiple offers, go with the offer you are most comfortable with. Obviously, you can only sell your home to one family!

One other significant variable that might help you make a decision in a multiple offer scenario is to discover the buyers' reason for wanting to purchase our home. Knowing this information will help you make a wise decision. Why do they want to live in that house? That is a really good question! If we have two people who both want the same house and one buyer wants to live in the house because his elderly parents live about three houses down and the other buyer wants to move in because he is getting evicted from his house next Tuesday and is panicking because he has nowhere to go, we probably want to pick the guy who wants to be near his parents. Pay close attention to the motivation of the buyer. Here are a few of the things we love to hear from buyers:

1. My two kids really want to keep going to the same schools and your house is in that district.
2. My aunt, cousin, brother, mom, or some other relative lives in the immediate area.
3. I grew up in this part of town and I will never leave this area.

4. I love this neighborhood and have been renting down the street for several years. It is time to get my own house and I love your home.
5. This is my dream house. I grew up in a house just like this down the street.

Remember, in a perfect world, someone would move into the house and pay every month for twenty years or more. When we have situations that make us feel like our home is just a temporary solution to their problem, it makes us a little cautious. Here are some of the things that buyers say that make us a little nervous:

1. My lease is up and I need a place to stay…quick! Can I move in by Friday?
2. I just went through a divorce and need to move out of my three-thousand-square-foot home with a pool into your one-thousand-square-foot home while I get back on my feet.
3. I just missed out on a much nicer home down the street but will settle for your home because my lease is up and I need to move within two weeks.
4. This house should hold us over for a couple of years and then we are going to need a much larger home.
5. This house will work for us, but I am probably getting transferred to California in the next few years.

We don't want the house to just "work" for the buyer. We want them to fall in love with the house and the area! Even though all of these buyers would put down a good down payment, we still like to do everything we can to ensure the buyer we choose really *wants* to be there and plans on being there for a long time. Nobody has a crystal ball and can predict the future, but we like to always stack the deck in our favor. Remember, finding a buyer is the *easiest* part of the process due to the huge demand for seller financing. Be patient and find the right buyer who you believe really wants to be in the house and plans on being there for a long time.

INTUITION-TRUST YOUR GUT FEELING

Story from Mike: *Several years ago my wife and I hired Mary, a cleaning lady to clean our home. Mary was as sweet as could be, and after her first cleaning, the home looked and smelled fantastic. I told my wife how happy I was with her work, and my wife said, "The house looks great, but there is something about her that makes me nervous." I was surprised by her comment and asked her what it was that she was concerned about. She kept telling me that she could not put her finger on it, but something made her nervous. We went ahead and let Mary keep coming to our house to clean about once a month for several months. One night after Mary had cleaned the house, we had plans for a birthday dinner with some close friends at a really nice restaurant. My wife went to her jewelry box to break out her diamond bracelet that she kept stashed away for special occasions. The bracelet was gone. I am not accusing Mary and would never accuse anyone unless I caught them in the act, but my wife instantly said, "I knew it!"*

Intuition is defined as "the act or faculty of knowing or sensing without the use of rational processes; immediate cognition." Intuition is an inner knowing, a gut feeling. It is often said that women tend to have more God-given intuition than men. Sometimes it is hard to put a finger on why something or someone doesn't "feel" right. In the seller-finance world, trust the feeling and run the other way if you are uncomfortable with a prospective buyer. There is a huge demand for seller financing. *Do not* sell a home to someone unless you have a good feeling about their character. You won't always be right, but God gave us intuition for a reason. Trust your gut; it is right more times than not.

Oftentimes that intuition or gut feeling is coming from the person's body language. It is a red flag when someone won't look us in the eye or looks down a lot during our conversations. This may be an indication that they have something to hide or are not being truthful. We are not body language experts, but we strongly encourage you to read up on body language tips and once again, trust your gut. More than 80 percent of communication is nonverbal. Even if the homebuyer is saying all the right things, which they will, trust your gut feeling more than anything else.

It takes more than one "date" to get a feel for someone's character. Make sure you set up a few dates before you agree to get "married." For the sake of this discussion, let's assume we met someone at a home for the very first time and they really liked it and wanted to go forward with the purchase. The next thing we typically do is give them an application to complete and schedule a time to meet again to review the application. Along with the standard loan application, we always ask them to provide us with at least three personal and three business references. We contact these references first to verify the phone numbers are valid and second to find out additional information about the buyer. This tool has been extremely helpful during the underwriting process, and having those phone numbers really comes in handy if we ever end up with a disconnected phone number for the borrower and need to track them down. Along with the references, we always make sure we ask for their current landlord's information so we can verify their rental payment history. Poor payment history at their prior residence usually means we are going to have issues with the house payments as well. Poor payment history? Find another buyer. (If a buyer filled out an official loan application, you must inform them in writing of your decision to decline their application. Be sure to consult with a mortgage attorney and comply with all licensing requirements prior to getting into the seller-finance business.)

When they come to their second date, we look at how completely and neatly their application was filled out, whether they had the supporting income documentation, and whether they were *on time*! Showing up on time is one of the most fundamental character traits that someone can demonstrate. It shows respect for other people's time. Jim Rohn taught us that "all disciplines affect one another." If someone is not disciplined to be on time for an appointment, there is a good chance they will not be on time paying their bills. If someone is sloppy and incomplete on their paperwork, there is a good chance that they will not take good care of their property.

ALL DISCIPLINES AFFECT ONE ANOTHER

Story from Mike: *From my insurance business days, I will never forget the look in the eyes of the company representatives who came by my office one after another over a three-month period. Apparently there was some new information that was discovered by the actuaries regarding the connection between someone's credit score and their driving habits, and they all looked and acted as though they had just discovered fire.*

What was the connection? In short, they discovered that people with bad credit tend to have more accidents. In other words, if you are sloppy with your bills, you are probably sloppy behind the wheel as well! All five of my companies quickly changed all of their underwriting rules and adjusted rates based upon credit score. Do you know how hard it was to tell people their rates went up due to their credit and not necessarily due to an accident or ticket? Ugh, that was the most painful year I ever had in the insurance business.

This is just another example of what our mentor, Jim Rohn, taught us about all disciplines affecting other areas of our lives. The great thing about this truth is that you can apply it to your life in a positive way. Did you ever notice when you start to exercise you tend to start eating better? Did you ever notice that when you start eating better you tend to sleep better? Focus on improving just one key discipline in your life and it will have a positive effect on all other areas.

DO CREDIT SCORES MATTER?

OK, let's get back to the underwriting process. Let's say that the prospective buyer showed up for the second date on time and with their paperwork in good order. We still schedule one more date before we make a decision to go forward. After we review their paperwork, we say something like this: "Everything looks good so far; thanks for bringing in your paperwork. The next step is for us to schedule a time a couple of days from now to sign the contract. In the meantime, we will be ordering your credit report, verifying the information on your application, and preparing the contract. We are not overly concerned about your credit score; we just want to make sure the information on your application is verified on your credit report."

Credit score is a sensitive issue for many people. We always reassure our buyers that their loan approval is not solely based on their credit score. We just want to make sure that the credit report "matches their story." By the way, there are services that will check credit for you for a reasonable fee and they are easy to find. Just Google "tenant screening services." Even though you are selling the home, these companies primarily help landlords but can help you screen your buyers as well.

When you focus on selling homes in the most affordable areas of your community, as we suggest with this business model, you will find that a large percentage of people might not have a credit score. We have found that many people live in a *cash only* world and simply do not use credit. We also see a large percentage of our buyers with low credit scores and almost everything on their credit report is medical bill related. Oftentimes, there was a legitimate health issue that really derailed them financially and crushed their score.

We believe basing an underwriting decision solely on a credit score is not wise. Our main focus when checking credit, once again, is to make sure the information on the credit report matches the story we are being told by the buyer and his loan application. If you do discover that the credit scores are really low, you may consider asking for a loan guarantor. It is the equivalent of having someone cosign for a car loan. You would be surprised at how many people are willing to get one of their relatives to step up and guarantee the loan.

This is extremely helpful when it comes time to sell the note. You can tell your note buyer, "The credit scores for the buyers were not too strong, but the wife's father agreed to be a loan guarantor. He had a seven hundred credit score and has been at the same job for twenty years." That is huge when you are trying to sell the note! Whenever you have a "weak" buyer, always try to get a solid loan guarantor.

With our character underwriting strategy and down payment criteria, we have consistently produced notes that perform 95 percent of the time. Our 5 percent default rate is among the best in the country and we continue to underwrite diligently to try to select the right buyers. *Never* be in a rush to get the first warm body into your house. Once you sign a contract and they move in, you are married to them for a long time. For better or worse!

DEBT TO INCOME RATIO

One other key factor to pay close attention to as you are trying to choose the right buyer is to pay close attention to their debt-to-income ratio (DTI). If someone makes $3,000 per month and their house payment is $1,000 per month, they have a DTI of 33 percent. Federal loan guidelines often recommend a DTI of 43 percent or less. Even if you have a buyer with a good down payment with good character, you are not doing them any favors by selling them a house they cannot afford. We recommend following the federal loan guidelines and making sure your buyers have a DTI of 43 percent or less.

Keep in mind, the philosophy driving this approach to underwriting is to take enough time to make sure you have a buyer who really wants the house, qualifies financially, and is willing to jump through a few hoops to get it. If someone is going to get cold feet and back out of a deal, now is the time. Trust us, if someone really wants the house, they will jump through a few hoops to get it.

On the third appointment, it is time to actually sign the contract to sell the house. We review their credit report and discuss the terms of the contract, including the fact that the home is sold *as is*. We had our attorney draft a special *as-is* addendum that the buyer must sign, acknowledging they are buying the home "with all its faults," etc. When someone calls us a year later griping about something wrong with the house, we often e-mail them a copy of the *as-is* form they signed. A copy of this form can be found on our website.

Unlike many traditional real estate transactions in which we have relatively small amounts of earnest money ($500 or $1,000), we require 50 percent of the estimated dollar amount needed to close on the property. This amount is usually a minimum of $5,000. We also explain that monthly payments must be deducted directly out of their checking account on the first of the month and make this a loan requirement. Most basic business checking accounts offer the ability to draft monthly payments from a borrowers' account. Remember, when you offer seller financing, you call the shots.

Assuming we get the 50 percent down and also the signed bank draft authorization form, we are feeling pretty confident that the transaction is on track for a smooth closing. This is also a great time to stress to your buyer that the home is sold "in its current condition" (that is a nicer way of saying *as is*) and recommend that they hire a home inspector so they know exactly what they are buying. It has been our experience that many home buyers choose *not* to hire a professional home inspector. The main reason is simply the cost. If they choose not to hire a home inspector, we encourage them to inspect the home themselves and spend as much time as they want testing out the plumbing, electrical, and anything else they desire.

After the contract is signed and the earnest money is delivered to the title company, it is time to do the loan disclosures. As we mentioned earlier in this book, we believe the best way to comply with all of the state and federal laws is to work with a mortgage company that will prepare the documents for you. Take a look at the following list of forms in a typical loan disclosure package and also the state and federal laws that govern the mortgage industry:

FEDERAL MORTGAGE FORMS AND LAWS

Forms:

Truth in Lending
Uniform Residential Loan Application
Notice to the Home Loan Applicant
Anti-Steering Disclosure—Fixed Loans
Fees Worksheet
Good Faith Estimate
Borrower Signature Authorization
Borrower's Certification and Authorization
Affidavit of Occupancy
Anti-Coercion Statement
Fair Credit Reporting Act
Equal Credit Opportunity Act
Homeownership Counseling Notice & Acknowledgment of Receipt
Mortgage Loan Origination Agreement
Mortgage Company Disclosure
Patriot Act Information Disclosure
Customer Identification Documentation Patriot Act
Notice of What Mortgage Company Does with Borrower's Personal Information
The Right to Receive Appraisal
Servicing Disclosure Statement
Intent to Proceed with Application
Notice of Penalties for Making False Statements

Federal and State Laws:

Regulation B: Equal Credit Opportunity Act (ECOA)
Regulation C: Home Mortgage Disclosure (HMDA)
Regulation F: Fair Debt Collection Practices Act

Regulation H: S.A.F.E. Mortgage Licensing Act—State Compliance and Bureau Registration System
Regulation Z
Fair Housing Act

In our online course, we have a complete lesson on presenting loan disclosures and go through all of the paperwork in a typical loan package. As you can see by the amount of paperwork and laws affecting a typical loan, it is wise to work with a mortgage company to produce all of the paperwork to ensure compliance with the law. Then you can focus on what you are good at: real estate!

Depending on the interest rates charged, your borrower may have to go through a pre-loan counseling session with a certified HUD loan counselor. Upon completion of this session, the borrower will receive a certificate that must be provided to you, the lender, prior to closing.

The final step prior to actually closing at the title company is to do a final walk-through with the buyer. Literally the day before or the day of closing, we like to meet the buyer at the home and walk through the property. We want to make sure that if there are any last-minute questions or issues they get addressed *before* the closing. Was the trash from the contractor hauled off? Does the yard need mowing one last time? Was the new ceiling fan that was promised installed and working? Is the hot water heater on and working? Is the water turned on at the meter? The goal of the walk-through once again is to make sure there are no loose ends prior to closing. There is actually a final walk-through form that we have the buyer sign. If there are any loose ends, there is a place on the form where we can list the items that need to be taken care of. There is also a section that they sign acknowledging whether or not they hired a professional inspector. When we do the walk-through, we are sure to remind them of the following four things:

1. The house is sold in its current condition.
2. They must transfer the utilities into their name on the day of closing.

3. They need to have scheduled an appointment with the title company and know exactly how much money they need to bring to closing. They must bring a cashier's check. Most title companies only want certified funds in the form of a cashier's check and will not accept cash or money orders.
4. Their first payment will be automatically drafted out of their bank account on the first of each month.

PRESENTING YOUR MORTGAGE TERMS TO THE BUYER

We have just a few other thoughts to share with you regarding character underwriting. First, character goes both ways. If you have high expectations from your borrower, they should have high expectations from you. Always be honest and disclose everything you know about the house. You should always complete a Seller's Disclosure Notice and let the buyer know everything that is wrong with the house as far as you know. Also, it is a federal law that you must disclose anything you know about lead-based paint on any home built before 1978. There is a Lead Base Paint addendum that needs to be attached to the Seller's Disclosure Notice if the homes was built prior to 1978. All of these forms are available on our website and we have an entire lesson in our online course dedicated to all of the paperwork needed to facilitate a real estate transaction both legally and ethically.

Along with fully disclosing the condition of the property to the buyer, we feel it is equally important to properly articulate the terms of the financing you are offering. If you create real estate notes using our system, these are the key points that should be covered with each and every buyer:

1. The interest rate is fixed. In other words, this is not an adjustable rate mortgage.
2. Your payment includes taxes and insurance. Since the principal and interest amount of your payment never changes (fixed), the only things that can affect your payment is a change in the property taxes or insurance.

3. There is no balloon payment. A balloon payment is when the entire balance is due in a certain period of time. For example, three years or five years. In other words, we are not going to force you to refinance. You can stay in the house thirty years and keep making your monthly payments if you choose to do so.
4. There is no prepayment penalty. In other words, if you decide to refinance a month from now or two years from now you can do so. There is nothing in our paperwork that prevents you or penalizes you for refinancing or paying off the loan early.
5. We are charging you an interest rate that is higher than a typical mortgage company and we sold you the house at market value. If you can refinance the house down the road and get a lower interest rate, your payments will go down. Many sellers who offer financing drastically inflate the sales price of the house above market value. This could cause a problem when you go to refinance. Once again, we sold you the home at a fair market value and you should have no problem getting it appraised if you get to a position where you can refinance.

We sleep well at night by presenting our loans in the way we just outlined above. The truth is, the monthly payment on the house usually shakes out to be about the same as the buyer was paying in rent. We have found that these buyers are generally thrilled with their house payments and the fact that they are paying 10 percent interest or more is a nonissue. We have been shocked by the small amount of buyers who have refinanced their loans. As of the writing of this book, it has literally been less than one per year! The bottom line is that the buyers are comfortable with their payments and sincerely appreciate the financing opportunity and usually just keep on making their payments.

SERVICE AFTER THE SALE

About 25 percent of the time, someone moves into the house and calls us in the next week or so to tell us about a problem: "My kitchen sink leaks; I have an electrical outlet that is not working; I found some trash that your contractor left behind my house; I had a tree branch fall in my front yard"...

and the list goes on and on. Most of the time, we believe the correct attitude and philosophy on these types of issues is to go ahead and try to get them addressed right away. Remember, you want to have a good relationship with your homeowners. They are the ones who are going to fill your mailbox with money month after month. Even though the homes are sold *as is*, if there is a minor issue that comes up shortly after closing, go ahead and address it. Every now and then, someone will try to take advantage of your cooperation and call you every week about some new issue. You need to remind them that this is not a rental and at some point, take a hard stance and say *no* to a repair request. Some people mistake niceness for weakness. Put your foot down when you come across someone with an entitlement mentality.

We got a call from a lady who purchased a home from us and had been living there for over six months. She said that her roof was leaking really badly and that sheetrock was falling in her kitchen and bedroom. We told her we did not do anything to the roof because it looked like it was in great shape and relatively new. We did not offer to fix the roof, but we did recommend a roofer to her. The roofer called us from the house and asked if we would come on down to take a look at something. When we arrived, the roofer let us know that the front half of the roof was almost brand-new and that the back half of the roof was about thirty years old. Evidently, the previous owner only had a budget for half of a roof. We never knew that only half of the roof was new. The only shingles that you could see were in the front of the house. The backyard was too small to get a good angle to see it and we had no reason to get up on the roof because we thought it was new and in great shape.

We had absolutely no obligation to do anything in this situation. The house was sold *as is* and the homeowner chose not to hire a professional inspector. We did, however, feel sorry for the homeowner. We chose to pay 50 percent of the cost of a new roof, and the homeowner was extremely appreciative and has never missed a single payment. We would like to think that our good deed played a small role in her perfect payment history.

One other tool you want to have in your owner-finance bag is flexibility. Several times a year, we will have a borderline buyer who makes us nervous for some reason or other. It might be something as simple as them having been at their job for only a very short time or their debt-to-income ratio is a little higher than normal. If this is the case, be a little flexible and creative. If we were shooting for 10 percent down and are uncomfortable with something on their application, instead of denying the application, we might consider going forward with 15 percent or 20 percent down instead of just 10 percent or we might try to get a loan guarantor. Try not to let the deal die on your side of the table. Always look for a way to make the deal work, especially if you have someone with good character and a solid down payment trying to purchase your home.

You did it! You sold your first house and created your first real estate note! Now you get to start collecting checks each month. In the next chapter we are going to talk about making sure those income streams keep rolling and what to do if there is a disruption to your income stream.

ERIK AND MIKE'S BOTTOM LINE:
Get a minimum of 10 percent down and take your time finding the right buyer. There is a huge demand for seller financing. Take enough time during the underwriting process to either promote or expose the buyer. Make sure his or her debt-to-income ratio is below 43 percent.

"Successful people move on their initiative, but they know where they are going before they start."

-Jim Rohn

9

BABYSITTING YOUR MAILBOX MONEY

Story from Erik: *It was a cold, rainy day and we hadn't purchased a property in more than two weeks! In the previous fourteen days we had looked at more than two hundred homes and made more than forty offers. All of them were rejected and we were in a serious buying drought.*

*Our cash was burning a hole in our pocket and we were determined to find a deal...*today*! Most of the homes we looked at were vacant, but we pulled into house number twenty-two and there was a car in the driveway. We were thrilled! If the owner was home we were going to try to make a deal right now! Even though it is totally against the rules to negotiate directly with the seller since they are represented by a Realtor, we were desperate for our real estate fix. (There are more destructive things to be addicted to than real estate!) We rang the doorbell and a man came to the door. We introduced ourselves and asked if he would give us a quick tour.*

After the tour, we asked the guy why he was selling. He said that he and his wife were struggling and he wanted to move to the West Coast for a fresh start. We asked whether he had a mortgage on his home and was current on his loan. He informed us that he had not made a payment in more than thirteen months! He also said he was not planning on moving until he got his foreclosure notice from the bank. In the meantime, he was enjoying "free rent" and stashing away cash for the move until the mortgage company came knocking. The guy owed too much to make a deal, so we quickly left and went on to house number twenty-three.

Whoever was handling the loan servicing definitely was not on top of their business. The guy had not paid in more than thirteen months and the foreclosure process had not even started! If you service your notes like this, you will go broke and lose your potential fortune. If you are going to be in the seller-finance business, you have to stay on top of your collection issues.

If you follow the steps taught in this book and our course to create real estate notes, income streams will start flowing into your bank account. In a perfect world, you would never hear from the home buyer again and the checks would just keep coming month after month and year after year. Unfortunately, we do not live in a perfect world. Checks bounce, people lose their jobs, get divorced, refinance and sell their homes. You can minimize the number of headaches and maximize the income stream by adopting the right attitude and philosophy toward loan servicing and keeping a short leash on collection issues.

Our philosophy on payment and collection issues is simple: We did our part by extending credit to a buyer who could not get traditional financing and they should do their part by making their monthly payments on time. If a payment is late or a check bounces, we communicate with the buyer and work with them as long as they are communicating and following through on their commitments. If we are dealing with someone who is not returning our calls and does not follow through on their promises, we quickly take the necessary legal steps to get them out of the house. It is really that simple. If you don't pay, you don't stay.

Before we get into the specifics of servicing notes, let's discuss the legal documents used to actually create a real estate note and the process of selling a note to an investor. Let's start with the legal documents that are typically produced by the real estate attorney that were signed at the closing at the title company.

LEGAL DOCUMENTS CREATING THE REAL ESTATE NOTE

1. **Promissory Note:** This document outlines the terms of the note such as the loan amount, interest rate, term of the loan, and penalties for late payments. This document holds all of the financial details of the repayment and the structure of the loan. This is not a recorded document and does not have to be notarized. Therefore, the true financial details of the transaction are not given to the public. Here is a sample of a Promissory Note template.

Promissory Note

Date:
Borrower:
Borrower's Mailing Address:
Lender:
Place for Payment:
Principal Amount:
Annual Interest Rate:
Maturity Date:
Annual Interest Rate on Matured, Unpaid Amounts:
Terms of Payment (principal and interest):
Security for Payment:
Other Security for Payment:

Promise to Pay

Borrower promises to pay to the order of Lender the Principal Amount plus interest at the Annual Interest Rate. This note is payable at the Place for Payment and according to the Terms of Payment. All unpaid amounts are due by the Maturity Date. If any amount is not paid either when due under the Terms of Payment or on acceleration of maturity, Borrower promises to pay any unpaid amount plus interest from the date the payment was due to the date of payment at the Annual Interest Rate on Matured, Unpaid Amounts.

Defaults and Remedies

If Borrower defaults in the payment of this note or in the performance of any obligation in any instrument securing or collateral to this note, Lender may declare the unpaid principal balance, earned interest, and any other amounts owed on the note immediately due.

Waivers

Borrower and each surety, endorser, and guarantor waive, to the extent permitted by law, all (1) demand for payment, (2) presentation for payment, (3) notice of intention to accelerate maturity, (4) notice of acceleration of maturity, (5) protest, [and] (6) notice of protest, and (7) rights under sections 51.003 and 51.004 of the Texas Property Code.

Attorney's Fees

Borrower also promises to pay reasonable attorney's fees and court and other costs if this note is placed in the hands of an attorney to collect or enforce the note. These expenses will bear interest from the date of advance at the Annual Interest Rate on Matured, Unpaid Amounts. Borrower will pay Lender these expenses and interest on demand at the Place for Payment. These expenses and interest will become part of the debt evidenced by the note and will be secured by any security for payment.

Usury Savings

Interest on the debt evidenced by this note will not exceed the maximum rate or amount of non-usurious interest that may be contracted for, taken, reserved, charged, or received under law. Any interest in excess of that maximum amount will be credited on the Principal Amount or, if the Principal Amount has been paid, refunded. On any acceleration or required or permitted prepayment, any excess interest will be canceled automatically as of the acceleration or prepayment or, if the excess interest has already been paid, credited on the Principal Amount or, if the Principal Amount has been paid, refunded. This provision overrides any conflicting provisions in this note and all other instruments concerning the debt.

Other Clauses

Each Borrower is responsible for all obligations represented by this note. When the context requires, singular nouns and pronouns include the plural.

______________________________ **[Name of borrower]**

2. **Deed of Trust**: This document names a "Trustee" who has the right to foreclose on the property if the borrower doesn't make their monthly payments. In some states the document that allows you to foreclose is called a Mortgage. This document gets recorded at the local county courthouse. Here is a sample of a Deed of Trust template.

Deed of Trust

Notice of confidentiality rights: If you are a natural person, you may remove or strike any or all of the following information from any instrument that transfers an interest in real property before it is filed for record in the public records: your Social Security number or your driver's license number.

Date:
Grantor:
Grantor's Mailing Address:
Trustee[s]:
Trustee's Mailing Address[es]:
Lender:
Lender's Mailing Address:
Obligation:
Note Date:
Original Principal Amount:
Borrower:
Lender:
Maturity Date:
Other Debt:
Property (including any improvements):
Prior Lien: [**include recording information**]
Other Exceptions to Conveyance and Warranty:

A. Granting Clause

For value received and to secure payment of the Obligation, Grantor conveys the Property to Trustee in trust. Grantor warrants and agrees to defend the title to the Property, subject to the Other Exceptions to Conveyance and Warranty. On payment of the Obligation and all other amounts secured by this deed of trust, this deed of trust will have no further effect, and Lender will release it at Grantor's expense.

B. Grantor's Obligations

B.1. Grantor agrees to maintain all property and liability insurance coverages with respect to the Property, revenues generated by the Property, and operations on the Property that Lender reasonably requires ("Required Insurance Coverages"), issued by insurers and written on policy forms acceptable to Lender, and as to property loss, that are payable to Lender under policies containing standard mortgagee clauses, and deliver evidence of the Required Insurance Coverages in a form acceptable to Lender before execution of this deed of trust and again at least ten days before the expiration of the Required Insurance Coverages.

B.2. Grantor agrees to—

1. keep the Property in good repair and condition;
2. pay all taxes and assessments on the Property before delinquency, not authorize a taxing entity to transfer its tax lien on the Property to anyone other than Lender, and not request a deferral of the collection of taxes pursuant to section 33.06 of the Texas Tax Code;
3. defend title to the Property subject to the Other Exceptions to Conveyance and Warranty and preserve the lien's priority as it is established in this deed of trust;
4. obey all laws, ordinances, and restrictive covenants applicable to the Property;
5. keep any buildings occupied as required by the Required Insurance Coverages;
6. if the lien of this deed of trust is not a first lien, pay or cause to be paid all prior lien notes and abide by or cause to be abided by all prior lien instruments; and
7. notify Lender of any change of address.

C. Lender's Rights

C.1. Lender or Lender's mortgage servicer may appoint in writing one or more substitute trustees, succeeding to all rights and responsibilities of Trustee.

C.2. If the proceeds of the Obligation are used to pay any debt secured by prior liens, Lender is subrogated to all the rights and liens of the holders of any debt so paid.

C.3. Lender may apply any proceeds received under the property insurance policies covering the Property either to reduce the Obligation or to repair or replace damaged or destroyed improvements covered by the policy. If the Property is Grantor's primary residence and Lender reasonably determines that repairs to the improvements are economically feasible, Lender will make the property insurance proceeds available to Grantor for repairs.

C.4. Notwithstanding the terms of the Note to the contrary, and unless applicable law prohibits, all payments received by Lender from Grantor with respect to the Obligation or this deed of trust may, at Lender's discretion, be applied first to amounts payable under this deed of trust and then to amounts due and payable to Lender with respect to the Obligation, to be applied to late charges, principal, or interest in the order Lender in its discretion determines.

C.5. If Grantor fails to perform any of Grantor's obligations, Lender may perform those obligations and be reimbursed by Grantor on demand for any amounts so paid, including attorney's fees, plus interest on those amounts from the dates of payment at the rate stated in the Note for matured, unpaid amounts. The amount to be reimbursed will be secured by this deed of trust.

C.6. **COLLATERAL PROTECTION INSURANCE NOTICE In accordance with the provisions of section 307.052(a) of the Texas Finance Code, the Beneficiary hereby notifies the Grantor as follows:**

(A) the Grantor is required to:

(i) keep the collateral insured against damage in the amount the Lender specifies;

(ii) purchase the insurance from an insurer that is authorized to do business in the state of Texas or an eligible surplus lines insurer; and

(iii) name the Lender as the person to be paid under the policy in the event of a loss;

(B) the Grantor must, if required by the Lender, deliver to the Lender a copy of the policy and proof of the payment of premiums; and
(C) if the Grantor fails to meet any requirement listed in Paragraph(A) or(B), the Lender may obtain collateral protection insurance on behalf of the Grantor at the Grantor's expense.

C.7. If a default exists in payment of the Obligation or performance of Grantor's obligations and the default continues after any required notice of the default and the time allowed to cure, Lender may—

a. declare the unpaid principal balance and earned interest on the Obligation immediately due;
b. exercise Lender's rights with respect to rent under the Texas Property Code as then in effect;
c. direct Trustee to foreclose this lien, in which case Lender or Lender's agent will cause notice of the foreclosure sale to be given as provided by the Texas Property Code as then in effect; and
d. purchase the Property at any foreclosure sale by offering the highest bid and then have the bid credited on the Obligation.

C.8. Lender may remedy any default without waiving it and may waive any default without waiving any prior or subsequent default.

D. Trustee's Rights and Duties

If directed by Lender to foreclose this lien, Trustee will—

D.1. either personally or by agent give notice of the foreclosure sale as required by the Texas Property Code as then in effect;

D.2. sell and convey all or part of the Property "AS IS" to the highest bidder for cash with a general warranty binding Grantor, subject to the Prior Lien and to the Other Exceptions to Conveyance and Warranty and without representation or warranty, express or implied, by Trustee;

D.3. from the proceeds of the sale, pay, in this order—

expenses of foreclosure, including a reasonable commission to Trustee;

to Lender, the full amount of principal, interest, attorney's fees, and other charges due and unpaid;

any amounts required by law to be paid before payment to Grantor; and to Grantor, any balance; and

be indemnified, held harmless, and defended by Lender against all costs, expenses, and liabilities incurred by Trustee for acting in the execution or enforcement of the trust created by this deed of trust, which includes all court and other costs, including attorney's fees, incurred by Trustee in defense of any action or proceeding taken against Trustee in that capacity.

E. General Provisions

E.1. If any of the Property is sold under this deed of trust, Grantor must immediately surrender possession to the purchaser. If Grantor fails to do so, Grantor will become a tenant at sufferance of the purchaser, subject to an action for forcible detainer.

E.2. Recitals in any trustee's deed conveying the Property will be presumed to be true.

E.3. Proceeding under this deed of trust, filing suit for foreclosure, or pursuing any other remedy will not constitute an election of remedies.

E.4. This lien will remain superior to liens later created even if the time of payment of all or part of the Obligation is extended or part of the Property is released.

E.5. If any portion of the Obligation cannot be lawfully secured by this deed of trust, payments will be applied first to discharge that portion.

E.6. Grantor assigns to Lender all amounts payable to or received by Grantor from condemnation of all or part of the Property, from private sale in lieu of condemnation, and from damages caused by public works or construction on or near the Property. After deducting any expenses incurred, including attorney's fees and court and other costs, Lender will either release any remaining amounts to Grantor or apply such amounts to reduce the Obligation. Lender will not be liable for failure to collect or to exercise diligence in collecting any such amounts. Grantor will immediately give Lender notice of any actual or threatened proceedings for condemnation of all or part of the Property.

E.7. Grantor collaterally assigns to Lender all present and future rent from the Property and its proceeds. Grantor warrants the validity and enforceability of the assignment. Grantor will apply all rent to payment of the Obligation and performance of this deed of trust, but if the rent exceeds the amount due with respect to the Obligation and the deed of trust, Grantor may retain the excess. If a default exists in payment of the Obligation or performance of this deed of trust, Lender may exercise Lender's rights with respect to rent under the Texas Property Code as then in effect. Lender neither has nor assumes any obligations as lessor or landlord with respect to any occupant of the Property. Lender may exercise Lender's rights and remedies under this paragraph without taking possession of the Property. Lender will apply all rent collected under this paragraph as required by the Texas Property Code as then in effect. Lender is not required to act under this paragraph, and acting under this paragraph does not waive any of Lender's other rights or remedies.

E.8. Interest on the debt secured by this deed of trust will not exceed the maximum amount of non-usurious interest that may be contracted for, taken, reserved, charged, or received under law. Any interest in excess of that maximum amount will be credited on the principal of the debt or, if that has been paid, refunded. On any acceleration or required or permitted prepayment, any such excess will be canceled automatically as of the acceleration or prepayment or, if already paid, credited on the principal of the debt or, if the principal of the debt has been paid, refunded. This provision overrides any conflicting provisions in this and all other instruments concerning the debt.

E.9. In no event may this deed of trust secure payment of any debt that may not lawfully be secured by a lien on real estate or create a lien otherwise prohibited by law.

E.10. If Grantor transfers any part of the Property without Lender's prior written consent, Lender may declare the Obligation immediately payable and invoke any remedies provided in this deed of trust for default. If the Property is residential real property containing fewer than five dwelling units or a residential manufactured home, this provision does not apply to (a) a subordinate lien or encumbrance that does not transfer rights of occupancy of the Property; (b) creation of a purchase-money security interest for household appliances; (c) transfer by devise, descent, or operation of law on the death of a co-Grantor; (d) grant of a leasehold interest of three years or less without an option to purchase; (e) transfer to a spouse or children of Grantor or between co-Grantors; (f) transfer to a relative of Grantor on Grantor's death; (g) a transfer resulting from a decree of a dissolution of marriage, a legal separation agreement, or an incidental property settlement agreement by which the spouse of Grantor becomes an owner of the Property; or (h) transfer to an inter vivos trust in which Grantor is and remains a beneficiary and occupant of the Property.

E.10. Grantor may not sell, transfer, or otherwise dispose of any Property, whether voluntarily or by operation of law, without the prior written consent of Lender. If granted, consent may be conditioned upon (a) the grantee's integrity, reputation, character, creditworthiness, and management ability being satisfactory to Lender; and (b) the grantee's executing, before such sale, transfer, or other disposition, a written assumption agreement containing any terms Lender may require, such as a principal pay-down on the Obligation, an increase in the rate of interest payable with respect to the Obligation, a transfer fee, or any other modification of the Note, this deed of trust, or any other instruments evidencing or securing the Obligation.

Grantor may not cause or permit any Property to be encumbered by any liens, security interests, or encumbrances other than the liens securing the Obligation and the liens securing ad valorem taxes not yet due and payable without the prior written consent of Lender. If granted, consent may be conditioned upon Grantor's executing, before granting such lien, a written modification agreement containing any terms Lender may require, such as a principal pay-down on the Obligation, an increase in the rate of interest payable with respect to the Obligation, an approval fee, or any other modification of the Note, this deed of trust, or any other instruments evidencing or securing the Obligation.

Grantor may not grant any lien, security interest, or other encumbrance (a "Subordinate Instrument") covering the Property that is subordinate to the liens created by this deed of trust without the prior written consent of Lender.

If granted, consent may be conditioned upon the Subordinate Instrument's containing express covenants to the effect that—

> the Subordinate Instrument is unconditionally subordinate to this deed of trust;
>
> if any action is instituted to foreclose or otherwise enforce the Subordinate Instrument, no action may be taken that would terminate any occupancy or tenancy without the prior written consent of Lender, and that consent, if granted, may be conditioned in any manner Lender determines;
>
> rents, if collected by or for the holder of the Subordinate Instrument, will be applied first to the payment of the Obligation then due and to expenses incurred in the ownership, operation, and maintenance of the Property in any order Lender may determine, before being applied to any indebtedness secured by the Subordinate Instrument;
>
> written notice of default under the Subordinate Instrument and written notice of the commencement of any action to foreclose or otherwise enforce the Subordinate Instrument must be given to Lender concurrently with or immediately after the occurrence of any such default or commencement; and in the event of the bankruptcy of Grantor, all amounts due on or with respect to the Obligation and this deed of trust will be payable in full before any payments on the indebtedness secured by the Subordinate Instrument.

Grantor may not cause or permit any of the following events to occur without the prior written consent of Lender: if Grantor is (a) a corporation, the dissolution of the corporation or the sale, pledge, encumbrance, or assignment of any shares of its stock; (b) a limited liability company, the dissolution of the company or the sale, pledge, encumbrance, or assignment of any of its membership interests; (c) a general partnership or joint venture, the dissolution of the partnership or venture or the sale, pledge, encumbrance, or assignment of any of its partnership or joint venture interests, or the withdrawal from or admission into it of any general partner or joint venturer; or (d) a limited partnership (i) the dissolution of the partnership (ii) the sale, pledge, encumbrance, or assignment of any of its general partnership interests, or the withdrawal from or admission into it of any general partner, (iii) the sale, pledge, encumbrance, or assignment of a controlling portion of its limited partnership interests, or (iv) the withdrawal from or admission into it of any controlling limited partner or partners. If granted, consent may be conditioned upon (a) the integrity, reputation, character, creditworthiness, and management ability of the person succeeding to the ownership interest in Grantor (or security interest in such ownership) being satisfactory to Lender; and (b) the execution, before such event, by the person succeeding to the interest of Grantor in the Property or ownership interest in Grantor (or security interest in such ownership) of a written modification or assumption agreement containing such terms as Lender may require, such as a principal pay-down on the Obligation, an increase in the rate of interest payable with respect to the Obligation, a transfer fee, or any other modification of the Note, this deed of trust, or any other instruments evidencing or securing the Obligation.

E.11. When the context requires, singular nouns and pronouns include the plural.

E.12. The term *Note* includes all extensions, modifications, and renewals of the Note and all amounts secured by this deed of trust.

E.13. This deed of trust binds, benefits, and may be enforced by the successors in interest of all parties.

E.14. If Grantor and Borrower are not the same person, the term *Grantor* includes Borrower.

E.15. Grantor and each surety, endorser, and guarantor of the Obligation waive, to the extent permitted by law, all (a) demand for payment (b) presentation for payment (c) notice of intention to accelerate maturity (d) notice of acceleration of maturity (e) protest, [and] (f) notice of protest [**include if applicable**], and (g) rights under sections 51.003, 51.004, and 51.005 of the Texas Property Code.

E.16. Grantor agrees to pay reasonable attorney's fees, trustee's fees, and court and other costs of enforcing Lender's rights under this deed of trust if this deed of trust is placed in the hands of an attorney [**include if the transaction is a secondary mortgage loan:** who is not an employee of Lender] for enforcement.

E.17. If any provision of this deed of trust is determined to be invalid or unenforceable, the validity or enforceability of any other provision will not be affected.

E.18. The term *Lender* includes any mortgage servicer for Lender.

E.19. Grantor represents that this deed of trust and the Note are given for the following purposes: [**list specific purposes**].

______________________________ [**Name of grantor**]

3. **Warranty Deed with Vendors Lien**: This is the document that actually transfers ownership of the property from the seller to the buyer. "With Vendors Lien" means that there is a lien retained on behalf of the seller. This document gets recorded at the local county courthouse. Here is a sample of a Warranty Deed with Vendors Lien template.

Warranty Deed with Vendor's Lien

Notice of confidentiality rights: If you are a natural person, you may remove or strike any or all of the following information from any instrument that transfers an interest in real property before it is filed for record in the public records: your Social Security number or your driver's license number.

Date:
Grantor:
Grantor's Mailing Address:
Grantee: Grantee's Mailing Address:
Consideration: Property (including any improvements): Reservations from Conveyance:
Exceptions to Conveyance and Warranty:

Grantor, for the Consideration and subject to the Reservations from Conveyance and the Exceptions to Conveyance and Warranty, grants, sells, and conveys to Grantee the Property, together with all and singular the rights and appurtenances thereto in any way belonging, to have and to hold it to Grantee and Grantee's heirs, successors, and assigns forever. Grantor binds Grantor and Grantor's heirs and successors to warrant and forever defend all and singular the Property to Grantee and Grantee's heirs, successors, and assigns against every person whomsoever lawfully claiming or to claim the same or any part thereof, except as to the Reservations from Conveyance and the Exceptions to Conveyance and Warranty.

The vendor's lien against and superior title to the Property are retained until each note described is fully paid according to its terms, at which time this deed will become absolute.When the context requires, singular nouns and pronouns include the plural.______________________________________

[**Name of grantor**]

____

[**Name of grantee**]

Now that you have a basic understanding of the legal forms used to create a real estate note, lets talk about the steps you need to take to sell a note to an investor.

FIVE STEPS TO SELL A NOTE

1. **E-mail wiring instructions to the note buyer:** We need to receive the funds from the note buyer prior to going forward with the note transfer paperwork. The transfer documents need to be recorded and the last thing you want to happen is for a note buyer to change his mind AFTER you already recorded the new documents. NEVER do the transfer documents until you have full payment for the note.
2. **Complete a Transfer of Note and Liens document and record it at the local county courthouse.** This document transfers the two recorded liens to the new note buyer. Both the Deed of Trust and the Warranty Deed with Vendor's Lien will have "recorded document numbers." These document numbers are included on the "Transfer of Note and Liens" document and then recorded at the local county courthouse. The new note buyer now has all of the rights that you originally had when the loan was made. (See template at the end of this section)
3. **Endorse the Real Estate Note over to the new note buyer by attaching an Allonge to the original Real Estate Note:** The Allonge is simply a document affixed to the Real Estate Lien Note as a bill of exchange, for the purpose of receiving additional endorsements for which there may not be sufficient space on the note itself. An endorsement written on the Allonge is deemed to be written on the note itself. The Allonge basically endorses the Real Estate Note over to the new note buyer. Think of it like endorsing a check over to someone else so that they can cash it.
4. **Send a letter to the borrower informing them of the new note and lien holder:** We typically handle all of the servicing on the notes we sell, so, from a buyer's perspective, nothing changes. Their payment

continues to be made to the same location and continues to get drafted from their account on the first of each month.

5. **Send an advisement to the property insurance company:** After the note is sold, we contact the property insurance company and ask them to change the mortgagee (the party carrying the mortgage or Deed of Trust). In the event of an insurance claim, the claim check from the insurance company will be made payable to the mortgagee and the borrower. In other words, the note holder has to endorse the check in order for the borrower to cash the check. This helps ensure the note holder is in the loop and has some control over the collateral securing the real estate note.

TRANSFER OF NOTE AND LIENS
(Sample)

EFFECTIVE DATE:

HOLDER OF NOTES AND LIEN:

HOLDER'S MAILING ADDRESS:

TRANSFEREE NAME AND MAILING ADDRESS:

NOTE:

DATE:
ORIGINAL PRINCIPAL AMOUNT: **$**
BORROWER:
LENDER:
UNPAID PRINCIPAL: **$**

NOTE AND LIEN ARE DESCRIBED IN THE FOLLOWING DOCUMENTS, RECORDED IN: Warranty Deed with Vendor's Lien dated recorded under Document Number in the Official Public Records of Real Property of Bexar County, Texas and Deed of Trust of even date recorded under Document Number in the Official Public Records of Real Property of Bexar County, Texas.

PROPERTY (including any improvements): **LOT, BLOCK, NEW CITY BLOCK, IN THE CITY OF, COUNTY, TEXAS, ACCORDING TO THE PLAT THEREOF RECORDED IN VOLUME, PAGE, DEED AND PLAT RECORDS OF COUNTY, TEXAS.**

For value received, Holder of Note and Lien transfers them to Transferee, warrants that the Lien is valid against the Property in the priority indicated, and represents that the unpaid principal and interest on the Note are correctly stated.

This transfer is without recourse on Holder of Note and Lien.

Holder of Note and Lien expressly waives and releases all present and future rights to establish or enforce the liens described in this instrument as security for payment of any future or other indebtedness.

When the context requires, singular nouns and pronouns include the plural.

____

____

By

STATE OF TEXAS

This instrument was acknowledged before me on ________________, by _______________________________on behalf of said company.

____

NOTARY PUBLIC, STATE OF TEXAS

Once the official transfer legal documents have been recorded, we create a very simple "Note Binder." This binder has the following information neatly organized:

PRESENTING A NOTE TO A PROSPECTIVE NOTE BUYER—NOTE BINDER

1. **Pictures:** We always like to provide pictures of the home that is securing the note.
2. **Legal documents that were recorded:** These include the Transfer of Note and Liens (if the note has already been sold) along with the Deed of Trust and Warranty Deed with Vendor's Lien.
3. **The original Real Estate Note and Allonge**
4. **Property insurance certificate:** This verifies insurance was paid in full for one year. We also include a Flood Certificate verifying the property is not in a flood zone. (If the property was located in a high-risk flood zone, then flood insurance would also be included.)
5. **Copy of a title commitment or title policy:** This shows the property has a clear title and that the transaction was closed at a title company.
6. **Copy of the official settlement statement from the title company:** This document has every expense charged to both the buyer and seller and verifies the down payment made by the borrower.
7. **Borrower information:** This section has a copy of the original loan application along with the supporting documentation provided by the borrower documenting income. If the borrower received pre-loan counseling from a certified HUD counselor, a copy of the certificate is included in this section of the note binder.

Note binders are a great way to present a Real Estate Note to a prospective note buyer. Along with all of the information mentioned above, we prepare a "Note Summary." This one-page simple form gives a brief overview of the note you are selling. If you do a good job educating prospective note buyers on the fact that your notes are secured by real estate and that you collected a significant down payment, they will have a hard time saying no to the double-digit yields you are offering them. We have so many requests from other investors asking to see how we put together our note binders that we recently made them available on our website for purchase.

Preliminary Note Summary

Property Address: **1234 Main Street, San Antonio, TX 78212**

Sales Price: **$77,500.00**

Cash from Borrower: **$10,046.75 ($6,000.00 Down + $4,046.75 *Est.* Closing Costs & Prepaids)**

Original Loan Amount: **$71,500.00**
Current Loan Amount: **$71,500.00**

Interest Rate: **11.9 percent**

Term: **30 years**

Borrower has ACH Debit: **Yes—first payment due 12/01/2015**

Projected Origination Date: **10/31/2015**

Est. Monthly Payment:

$729.96 P&I
$129.22 Taxes
<u>$58.33 Insurance</u>
$917.51 TOTAL

Profile—Buyer: An established, married couple. He is in his fifties and has been working as a medical technician for over twenty-five years. She is in her forties and runs a permanent booth at the Mission Open Air Market. Combined, they have a low Debt-to-Income ratio of just 19.2 percent.

Profile—Property: This three-bedroom home is in a high-demand southeastern San Antonio neighborhood. The home has new paint, new lighting fixtures, updated kitchen cabinets, and beautifully refinished wood floors.

SERVICE AFTER THE SALE

Once a note is sold and we continue to handle the servicing, these are the steps we take each month:

1. We collect the payment from the borrower. Remember, we make it a loan requirement to have the payments drafted out of the borrowers' account on the first of every month.
2. On about the fifteenth of the month, the principal and interest portion of the payment collected is electronically transferred to the note holder. The taxes and insurance portion of the payment is then deposited into a separate escrow account. It is our fiduciary responsibility to keep those funds in a separate account so that when property taxes and insurance are due, we have the funds to pay them.
3. We notify the note holder by e-mail one business day prior to electronically transferring their payment. The e-mail also includes an actual "payment history" printout from our servicing software, which shows the exact day we posted the payment as well as the breakdown of the principal, interest, taxes, and insurance.

Assuming the borrower is paying on time, this system hums along just great. If a borrower bounces a check and we are dealing with a collection issue, we send an e-mail to our note holders informing them of the situation. Communication is key when working with your note holders. We have found that most note buyers are extremely patient and understanding when dealing with collection issues as long as you are keeping them in the loop. Most guys and gals who can afford to write multiple checks for $80,000 to purchase notes have been around the block a time or two. They understand that we don't live in a perfect world and collections are just part of the game.

At the end of the year in December we provide all of our investors with an **ACCOUNT VALUATION** document. This document shows the total loan balance that is still owed to the investor. The IRS requires that they document the value of all their assets at the end of the year in their IRA. Because many of our investors are holding their notes in their IRAs, we simply send the **ACCOUNT VALUATION** out to everyone.

In January we send out another **ACCOUNT VALUATION,** which is the actual year-end report for tax reporting. This document shows a summary of their account. It includes the service fees they paid, principal, interest, taxes, and insurance collected. The most important figure for the investor to receive is their interest income collected for the entire year. They are required by the IRS to report this on their income tax report. Note servicing software should easily be able to produce these reports.

Let's switch gears and take a look at a few common servicing situations so we can share with you our servicing philosophy and keep your streams of income on track. As you communicate with your borrowers about any issues whatsoever, be sure to take written notes and document the details of the conversation and keep them in your file. Be sure to make a note of the date and time you spoke.

NOTE SERVICING PHILOSOPHY—WHEN THINGS GO WRONG

1. Someone calls you for a repair issue after you already sold the house: It would be easy to have this attitude: "I am just the bank. Why are you calling me about your leaky kitchen sink?" Even though homes are sold *as is*, a high percentage of people still will call you about a problem they have with the house. Remember, in the homeowners' eyes, you are not "just the bank." You loaned them the money to buy the house AND sold them a renovated property. We are not suggesting that you should pay for every issue, but at the very least, listen to their problem and try to offer them a solution. Maybe you give them a number of a good plumber or maybe you call a plumber for them and choose to pay for it yourself. As a rule of thumb, we are generally willing to do something that will cost us about $200 or less if it comes up shortly after the homebuyer moves in *and* we think that it

was something that should have been addressed during the renovation process. Things like leaky kitchen sinks, slow-draining tubs, toilets that don't flush right, trash that wasn't hauled off, doors that don't close right, touch-up paint, etc.

We address these concerns because we want the homeowners to cheerfully send us money each month. Addressing minor issues can really help start the relationship off on the right foot. If we pay to solve a problem for someone, we usually say something like this: "John, all of our houses are sold as is and we normally don't deal with any repair issues. This is not a rental home. You own your house and we are just doing the financing for you. People don't call Wells Fargo when they have a problem with their toilet. We took care of this issue for you because we really like you and your family and we know that you just had a lot of moving expenses and wanted to get our relationship off on the right foot." We want the borrower to feel like we made a special exception for them. Do what you can to keep a good relationship with the people writing you checks.

2. Late payments: Once a payment is more than fifteen days late, we pick up the phone and give a courtesy call to check the status of the payment. Most of the time, we are told "the check is in the mail" or "I will drop it off on Friday." The challenge with making courtesy calls is that if you call too often, your borrowers will get in the habit of waiting for your call before they make the payment. We suggest calling no more than two months in a row to avoid "training" them to pay only after you call. If the payments do not get paid on time for two months in a row, we no longer call. We just send out a late notice and charge them a late fee. Many people consistently pay the late fee and, quite frankly, we have no problem with this as long as their payment gets submitted within the current month that it is due.

   One of the best strategies you can use to minimize late payments is to make it a loan requirement to have monthly payments drafted directly out of their bank accounts. This strategy is not bulletproof because automatic payments can still bounce. However, this has drastically reduced the number of bounced checks that we have had to deal with over the years. Oftentimes, we have had customers refuse to sign an authorization to draft their accounts and guess what? We refuse to sell them the house. That is the beautiful thing about offering seller-financing terms. There is a huge demand, and if the potential buyer does not want to play by your rules, someone else will.

Most banks provide the tools to easily and affordably draft payments from your borrowers' bank accounts. If you get a notice from your bank that an attempted bank draft "bounced," contact the borrower immediately and request that they drop off a payment or send it via overnight mail. *Do not* "redraft" the payment on another day. We explain to our customers that payments only get drafted on the first of the month and we do not draft any other days of the month. There is a cost to drafting payments and the last thing you want to do is let your borrowers think they can tell you the date they want their payment made each month.

During the underwriting process when we explain our payment procedures, we often get comments like, "I get paid on the third of each month," or "I get paid every Friday and sometimes it falls after the first." Our response is always the same: "If you get one month ahead in your bank account, having your payment drafted on the first of the month will never become an issue." If we get a "deer in the headlights" look, we just look for another buyer. If a homebuyer does not have enough cash reserves in the bank on a consistent basis, they have no business buying a house, and we have no business selling them one. Some people should just be renters.

3. Disconnected phone numbers: Not having a valid phone number when you really need to contact a borrower is frustrating. If you did a good job during the underwriting process, you got every phone number and e-mail address of theirs that you could get your hands on. Also, you had at least a handful of personal and business references

with phone numbers as well. If you have a disconnected phone number and then try e-mail and get no response, pick up the phone and call some of their references. You would be shocked at how fast you get a phone call. Let's say you have a bounced check and don't have a valid phone number for the borrower. We would call every reference they gave us and say something like this: "We have been unable to contact John Smith and we are calling you because he gave us your number as a reference when he purchased the house. We have an important business matter to discuss with him regarding his home purchase. Can we pass along our number to you in case you happen to see or hear from him?" Nine out of ten times we get a call that same day. Be sure not to give out specific information to the references. Just let them know that you have been unable to reach them by phone and you have a "business matter to discuss."

4. More than sixty days late: Let's say one of your borrowers bounced a payment on June 1. You called them right away and they said they would be in on Friday with a cashier's check. Friday comes and goes and no payment is made. Now they are avoiding your phone calls. If this situation continues on for the full month of June with no replacement check, we then try to draft the July 1 payment. It usually takes less than a week for our bank to notify us of a bounced bank draft. If the July payment also bounces, we continue trying to contact the homebuyer and also reach out to their references again. Once they are two months behind and their third payment is due, we contact our attorney to send out a letter.

   The first letter the attorney sends to a delinquent borrower is what we call a "twenty-day letter." The letter documents the total amount due and gives the borrower twenty days to pay all of the money due in full. In this case it would include the June, July, and the August payments, late fees, NSF check fees and attorney fees. (Our attorney charges $300 for sending the letter.) This letter also states that if they do not pay the full amount due within the twenty days, we intend to proceed with foreclosure *and accelerate their debt*! Did you hear that? **If they don't pay their entire late balance in full within twenty days, we are no longer going to continue to accept monthly payments. That is what "accelerate their debt" means.** In other words, if the loan balance is $75,000 and they don't pay their late balance within the twenty days, you are going to send them a notice that they owe you the $75,000 *in full! No more payments*! The loan documents that the borrower signed at closing gives the lender (you) the right to *accelerate* the debt if the borrower does not honor the terms of the contract and pay as agreed. Usually, when you clearly communicate this fact to the borrower, they quickly find a way to scrape up the money and pay their past due balance.

5. Foreclosure Notice: Your borrower has missed a total of three payments and you sent them the "twenty-day" certified letter informing them that you are going to accelerate the debt and foreclose on the property. The twenty days came and went and you still have not received a payment. Assuming the borrower is now delinquent four months, it is time to send the "twenty-one-day" letter. We call it the twenty-one -day letter because you need to give the borrower a minimum twenty-one-day notice before you can legally foreclose. This notice is also sent via certified mail and a copy is also sent to the county clerk. In Texas, foreclosure auctions are held on the steps of the county courthouse on the first Tuesday of each month. Be sure to visit with a good local real estate attorney in your area to be sure you are complying with the foreclosure procedures in your state. Once the official foreclosure notice has been sent, the following five scenarios could take place:
    1. The borrower brings you a check in full for the entire note balance, late payments, late fees, and attorney fees. (This rarely happens.)
    2. The borrower never contacts you, and the trustee (person handling the foreclosure) shows up on the courthouse steps on the first Tuesday of the month and auctions off the property. About 95 percent of the time, homes auctioned off on the courthouse

steps do not have enough equity for investors to bid on them. Usually the trustee ends up "buying the property back" on behalf of the lender (you) at a price equal to the amount owed by the borrower. If this happens, you now legally own the house again. If another investor does bid above the pay-off amount, they must pay the money immediately and your trustee will collect the money on the spot.

3. The borrower contacts you prior to the foreclosure date and offers to pay all of the back payments, late fees, and attorney fees but cannot pay the entire accelerated loan balance. If this happens and you feel confident that the stream of income will be back on track, your real estate attorney can prepare a document called a "Loan Modification and Reinstatement," which basically puts things back the way they were prior to the foreclosure notice. In other words, you agree to go ahead and start accepting monthly payments again.
4. The borrower contacts an attorney and files for bankruptcy prior to the foreclosure date. If this happens, the foreclosure process is temporarily halted. The times that we have had to deal with a bankruptcy situation, the delinquent payments become part of the bankruptcy plan and get paid out over a number of years. All future mortgage payments are expected to be made per the terms of the real estate note.
5. The borrower communicates with you and is willing to move out before the scheduled foreclosure date. **This is by far the best and most cost-effective option.** We call this a "Deed in Lieu of Foreclosure." The borrower is signing over the deed to you, the lender, instead of going through the foreclosure process. Think of it as a voluntary repossession on a car. You take the car back to the dealership and hand them the keys. More than 90 percent of our foreclosure situations have been "Deeds in Lieu of Foreclosure." This avoids some legal expenses and saves everyone time and money. We have our attorney prepare the paperwork and also pay

a title company to do a title search to make sure no liens have been placed on the property. If there are liens on the property *you must go through the foreclosure process* to "clean up" the title.

Whenever we agree to do a Deed in Lieu of Foreclosure we make sure the borrower vacates the property prior to the scheduled foreclosure date. If they don't move out on time, we go ahead and instruct the trustee to go forward with the foreclosure. We have had situations in which a borrower is cooperating and is willing to move out but truly does not have the money to make the move. In these cases, we offer the borrowers "Cash for Keys."

We tell the borrower, "If you can be out by Friday, we will give you $300 to help with your moving expenses. Hopefully this will help you out. We either need to pay the money to the attorney for the foreclosure or we can pay it to you. Also, it keeps a foreclosure off of your credit report."

This strategy works extremely well and is truly a win-win for both parties. The best philosophy to have when facing foreclosure situations is to remember that time is money and the sooner you get someone out of the home who is not paying, the sooner you can get your stream of income back on track.

All of this foreclosure and bankruptcy talk can cause you to get a little nervous about lending money and holding real estate notes. The truth is, on our most recent $10,000,000 of notes generated; we have only had eight foreclosure situations. Seven of them ended up being Deeds in Lieu and we made money on every one of the situations when we resold the homes. Remember, you are the one doing the underwriting and choosing whom you sell your homes to. If you character underwrite and collect enough money down, you will have minimal problems with your mailbox money and always be in a position of strength.

The number one thing that made us dive into this business head first is the fact that if there is a problem, we can roll up our sleeves and fix it. Unlike some of the stock market and oil well investments we have made in the past, with real estate notes we have a great deal of control over what happens if something goes wrong. We are quite sure that many people reading this book have had that helpless feeling when their stock portfolio was crashing and they had no control. Those days are over! Investing in real estate notes **GIVES YOU CONTROL** if something goes wrong. If someone quits paying you, call the attorney and start the legal process. Your income stream will usually be back on track in a few short months. If a stock plummets, I guess you could try to call the CEO and ask him to wire some money into your brokerage account. Good luck on that one!

A man called our office a while back and requested an appointment to meet with us. He said he was new to the area and wanted to learn more about the owner-finance business. He told us his father had passed away about eighteen months earlier and had left him ten real estate notes in his will. He was an only child and his mother had passed away years earlier. Apparently he had not had a good relationship with his father and knew very little about the real estate business. When the attorney handling the estate probated the will, the son ended up with the real estate notes. When he started collecting the ten payments each month, he decided he was rich enough to quit his job and go do some traveling. The average payment was about $800 per month and $8,000 a month is the most he had ever made in his life. He was a single man and for almost a year he went on trip after trip. He also bought a new car. Life was great! Every month he would go to his mailbox and pick up ten checks. One way or another, he found a way to spend the $8,000 each month. The reason he had stopped by our office was to get some advice because one of his borrowers had stopped paying and he wanted to know how to handle the situation.

DON'T SPEND THE ESCROW MONEY

He said he had tried to contact the homeowner but did not have any good phone numbers for them. We talked about the foreclosure process and we referred him to a real estate attorney. During the conversation, we asked him about the taxes and insurance on the homes. He looked at us with a blank stare and said, "I guess the homeowners take care of that stuff." We asked him to bring us a copy of his files so we could review them. The next day, he walked into our office with a stack of ten files. As we studied the paperwork, we realized that the $800 payments *included taxes and insurance*! We asked him if he had been setting the tax and insurance portion of the payment aside in a separate account to pay when the bills came due. He gave us the same blank stare. Evidently, he had not paid the taxes or insurance for almost two years! He spent every dime of that money! The meeting turned into a two-hour free education course on owner financing and the note business. The short version of the story is that the guy ended up going back to work and it took him a couple of years to dig himself out of that mess.

The moral of the story is obviously to separate the principal and interest from the escrow amount. Remember, *the escrow money is not yours to keep or spend.* These funds are to be set aside in a *separate bank account* so that when the taxes and insurance come due, you have the money to pay them. If you do not have the discipline to segregate the escrow payments, *do not* get into the seller-finance business. Banks, investors, and auditors all want to know if you are honoring your fiduciary responsibility by keeping the escrow funds in a separate account *and* paying the taxes and insurance in a timely manner. As you know, taxes and insurance rates can go up or down. Each year, once you know what the property taxes and insurance premiums are, you need to make sure that you are collecting the correct amount each month. The goal is to have no more than two additional months of taxes and insurance held in escrow at any given time. After you pay the taxes and insurance, if you happen to have additional money that you are holding in escrow, it is your fiduciary responsibility to send the overage to the borrower. Once again, this is a fluid thing and it can change year by year. Be sure to consult with a local attorney to make sure you are complying with state and federal mortgage laws.

BECOME A SUCCESSFUL LOAN SERVICER

Here are a few other keys to being a successful loan servicer. First of all, you need a good software package to keep track of principal and interest, send out late notices, etc. When we first got into the business, someone recommended a software package called NoteSmith. We purchased the software and hit the ground running. Most note-servicing software companies offer a free demo so you can take the software for a test-drive. Be sure to find a company that has been around for a while and one that will help you over the phone when issues come up. One of the companies that has had very good review and we are in the process of checking out is The Mortgage Office. You can contact them at TheMortgageOffice.com or 800-833-3343.

One of the ways you can provide A-plus service to your borrowers is to be sure to pay their property taxes by the end of the calendar year. Even though there may not be a penalty to pay taxes in January of the following year, if you pay them by the end of December, your borrowers can write off the taxes on their current tax return. Also, each year you will have to send out a 1098 "interest paid" statement to all borrowers. You have until the end of January to send out the 1098 statements.

Regarding property insurance, remember, it was required that the buyer pay the insurance IN FULL for one year. The way to make certain this gets done is to have the insurance agent send a bill for an annual premium directly to the title company. If it is handled this way, the title company makes certain they collect the full annual premium from the buyer at the time of closing.

Insurance companies in general can be a real pain in the backside! We have learned over the years that many companies/agents will insure a home on the day of closing and then cancel the policy because when they finally got around to looking at the house, they found something that they did not like. The roof might have looked "older" or the home had asbestos siding. (Half of the homes on the south side of San Antonio have asbestos siding!) Also, many companies will give a really good price the first year and then their rates increase on renewal. Even if there were no claims! Over the years, we have learned that some companies like to insure older homes and some do not.

People are often surprised when they call a "brand name" company and get a price that is double what the premium would be with most other companies. Some of the "big boys" will give you a quote, but you better be ready to ante up! This has been our experience on selling homes under $100K. If your buyer is looking to you for advice on insurance, suggest that they call several companies, and encourage them to pay close attention to their coverage and deductible.

If you are going to get into the business of creating and selling real estate notes, you need to become a licensed Mortgage Loan Originator. You can take the classes online and then you have to take a test. It is a relatively painless and inexpensive process. Once you are licensed, you have to do continuing education on a regular basis to keep your license active. I know many "old school" investors who fly under the radar and do not have licenses. Our philosophy is this: We don't want to be looking over our shoulder worrying about whether or not someone is going to come knocking on our door someday because we are breaking the law. The people who step up and play by the rules are the ones who will ultimately build long-term wealth and sleep well at night. The federal agency that handles the licensing is the Nationwide Mortgage Licensing System (NMLS). Just Google *NMLS* and you will easily find the website.

We would like to close this chapter with a few simple suggestions on a system to reach out to your borrowers with some positive energy:

1. Deliver a closing gift to the buyer on the day they close. Go to your local grocery store, and put together a bag with some paper towels, cleaning supplies, trash bags, etc. Then go by a local pizza joint and get them a gift card for a free pizza.
2. Write a Personal Acknowledgement Note (PAN) shortly after the transaction is finalized and the buyer moves into the home. This is not just a "Thank you for your business" note. Think of it as a thank you note on steroids. The idea of a PAN is to refer to something that

happened during the course of your dealings with the buyer and acknowledge a character trait in the note. Here is an example of one that we sent out recently:

"John and Debra, congratulations on the purchase of your new home. When we met, we could tell by the reaction of your children's faces how excited they were to have a new home. You are both obviously fantastic parents, and we are so happy for you. We sincerely appreciate how cooperative you were throughout the entire home-buying process. We wish you all of the best and God bless you and your family."

Notice that we acknowledged them as being good parents and also very cooperative throughout the process. We can't begin to tell you the number of people who have received these notes and then stopped by our office at a later time. They walk in and act like lifelong friends due in part to a small *handwritten* note. Don't underestimate the power in this one!

3. Send an anniversary and birthday card to everyone in the family. The anniversary card is referring to the date that they closed on their home. Send them a card that reminds them that one year ago today, they purchased their home. Regarding birthday cards, you will have the buyer's birthdate on the loan application. Try to get the kids birthdates throughout the buying process as well and send them a card as well. Everyone likes getting birthday cards!
4. Send them a Thanksgiving card. Everyone sends Christmas cards but how many people send you a Thanksgiving card? Write a handwritten message inside the card letting them know that you are thankful that you met them and that they purchased one of your homes.

Setting up systems and following them pay huge dividends and develop amazing goodwill over time. In the following chapter, we are going to focus on working with the guys and gals with money. You need them and they need you!

ERIK AND MIKE'S BOTTOM LINE:

Keep a short leash on all collection issues and be sure to communicate frequently with your note buyers. If you have a collection situation and you can't seem to get a borrower on track, turn it over to the real estate attorney and don't lose any sleep over it. There is huge demand for owner financing and once the problem payer is out, there will be people standing in line to purchase the home.

"Your mental attitude is the medium by which you can balance your life and your relationship to people and circumstances...to attract what you desire.

"We are all born equal in the sense that we all have equal access to the Great Principle: the right to control our thoughts and mental attitude. A positive mental attitude is the greatest of life's riches...it is through this attitude that anything worthwhile is achieved.

"Keep your mind on the things you want and off the things you don't want. Remember the old proverb: 'Be very careful what you set your heart on, for you will surely achieve it.'"

—*Napoleon Hill*

10

EVERYONE NEEDS A MONEY MAN OR MONEY WOMAN

This chapter focuses on teaching you how to build relationships with private lenders, develop a network of individual note buyers, and how to build solid banking relationships. If you work hard and do what we teach you in this book, chances are you will end up very wealthy down the road. The key to getting wealthy is to stay focused on constantly improving and making sure that you have a clear vision of your goal. Remember to "begin with the end in mind." Our vision has always been to create massive streams of passive income that would not only take care of our daily living expenses but also provide us with enough cash to do anything we want in life. Everyone defines success in his or her own way. Use what we teach you in this book to move one step closer to *your* definition of success. For one person success might be making $5,000 per month in passive income and for another person the number might be $200,000 per month. Either way, we want to help equip you to continue moving in the direction of your goals.

According to the National Endowment for Financial Education, approximately 70 percent of people who come into unexpected large sums of money end up broke within seven years. Also, statistics show that 78 percent of all professional football players end up filing bankruptcy within five years of retiring. Even though a large percentage of these players have earned more in one year than most people do in a lifetime, they still end up broke.

Our business model—the same one we are teaching you—will make you wealthy if you stay the course and put the pieces of the puzzle together. However, if you do not have the proper money skills and money beliefs, you could get derailed along the way and end up broke.

A *belief* can be defined as "a feeling of certainty about what something means." The challenge with many of our beliefs is that they were given to us from other people or they were based on improper interpretations of past experiences. Did you know you can consciously decide what to believe? In order to do this you have to have specific references or experiences to support the belief. Let's say, for example you believe that you are intelligent. Why do you believe that? Maybe in school you got good grades and your parents always told you that you were smart and picked up new things easily. Therefore you "believe" you are intelligent.

We really want you to examine your beliefs about money and your ability to be successful. If you honestly believe you *will* be successful and that you *will* attract money people, guess what? *You will!* If you develop a sense of certainty about your beliefs and they are the right beliefs, there is nothing you cannot do. Even things other people believe are impossible. Beliefs are like a tabletop and the supporting references for those beliefs are the legs of the table.

> ***"Both poverty and riches are the offspring of thought. When faith is added to thought, the subconscious mind instantly picks up the vibration, translates it into its spiritual equivalent, and transmits it to Infinite Intelligence. Faith is the only agency through which the force of Infinite Intelligence can be harnessed and used.***
>
> ***"You can do it if you believe you can."***
>
> —*Napoleon Hill*

Here are some of our core beliefs and philosophies about money and business that we choose to believe and have served us well:

1. The only way to earn money is to bring **value** to the marketplace. With the owner-finance business model, we bring **value** by providing a clean, updated home at a fair price to our home buyers. For our private investors, we bring huge **value** by delivering and servicing a note that pays double-digit monthly returns. To our students, we mentor them and teach the philosophies, attitudes, and strategies that have made us successful. Even if they decide never to buy their first investment property, they can become educated and sophisticated note buyers because they thoroughly understand our business model.
2. If you become an expert at something, people will recognize this fact and be willing to lend you money. You can't fake becoming an expert; there are no shortcuts. Whether you choose the real estate model taught in this book or pick another path, become an expert in your specific niche. Read the books, take the courses, and study the laws. Jim Rohn used to say, "Time either promotes you or exposes you." You might be able to fake it for a while, but if you have not done your homework, your money people will soon figure out you are incompetent and stop lending you money.
3. Proverbs 21: 5 says, "The plans of the diligent lead to profit as surely as haste leads to poverty." Build your wealth slowly over time. That is how you get rich. In today's instant microwave world, everyone is looking for shortcuts. Get rich the old-fashioned way: work hard, be patient, and persevere.
4. Once again, Jim Rohn taught us to "Be happy with what you have while in pursuit of what you want." This is one of the absolute best philosophies on the planet and bears repeating. Be just as happy when you start your wealth journey as when you actually arrive at your destination. Being happy is a choice. Pursue your dreams and become all you can be, *but* make sure you enjoy the ride! Too many

people are miserable along the way as they pursue their goals. Once they achieve them, they don't know how to enjoy themselves. Life is a journey, not a destination.

5. Another one of Jim's philosophies regarding money already presented in a previous chapter also bears repeating: Set a goal to become a millionaire but not just for the money. Become a millionaire "...for what it will make of you to achieve it." Jim also used to talk about people who had the attitude "Why work that hard? Why study so much? Why read all of those books and take all of those classes? Jim's answer was simple: *Why not?* Why not become a millionaire? Why not read more books? Why not shoot for the stars? Why not *you* and why not *now*? What else are you going to do with your time, watch another hour of garbage on television?
6. Here are some other empowering quotes, from Anthony Robbins, that will help you stay on the path to personal and financial success:
   a. "The past does not equal the future."
   b. "There is always a way if I am committed."
   c. "There are no failures, only outcomes. As long as I learn something I am succeeding."
   d. "Everything happens for a reason and a purpose that serves me."
   e. "I give more of myself than anyone expects."

Carefully think about and work on developing the right attitudes and philosophies toward success. Remember, philosophy is the foundation of sustained success. Read Chapter 1 on the psychology of a millionaire investor until the principles infiltrate every fiber of your being. Too many people just try to work on the mechanics of a business without putting any energy into their philosophy. Mechanics *and* philosophy work in perfect harmony to produce outstanding results.

Before we dive into the subject of private lenders, let's assume you have a long list of reasons why you think you won't be able to find someone to lend you money or why you can't pull the trigger on your first real estate deal. Maybe you believe you are too young or too old or that you do not have enough experience. Remember what we said earlier in No. 2 above, if you become an expert in something, people will find *you* and be willing to lend you money to support your vision. This is where you should focus your energy. Focus on becoming an expert and learning everything you can about your niche in the real estate business. After you have the knowledge, *take action*! You can't go to YouTube and learn how to ride a bike or swim. Eventually you have to jump in the pool!

RICE AND BEANS

The best-case scenario and our recommendation before you start talking to private investors is to save enough money to do at least one successful real estate deal on your own. There is nothing that replaces the real-life experience of working hard and saving money and then investing that money into a successful real estate transaction and turning a nice profit. Guess what? If you do it once, you can do it over and over again! That is all we have done, and we have created millions and millions of dollars in notes. It all started with the very first one. Then we *believed* we could do it and started talking to private money people to accelerate our growth. There is nothing more powerful than when you show a private investor you know what you are doing and you know how to make a profit.

> ***"Dishonest money dwindles away, but he who gathers money little by little makes it grow."***
>
> ***—Proverbs 13:11***

If you have not saved up much cash, you must be willing to sacrifice almost everything when you are trying to get some money together to do your first deal. Save, save, save, and eat rice and beans, as financial author Dave Ramsey says. Get a full-time job and two part-time jobs. Pop in at your parents and friends homes about dinnertime on a regular basis. Ride your bike instead of burning gas. Sell things you don't need. *Do whatever it takes!* Few things are more satisfying than paying *cash* for your first investment property knowing that you earned and saved every penny. Remember, you are not doing this just for one small profit on one small real estate deal. Keep focused on the big picture. That first transaction is the first step toward an amazing journey building massive passive streams of income.

DUDE, THAT'S MY CAR

When you are working on a goal, you need to consciously program your subconscious mind. Earl Nightingale said "The mind moves in the direction of our currently dominant thought." Scientists will tell you that this method works because of the reticular activating system in our brain, which acts like an antenna or radar that attracts things we focus on. Have you ever purchased a new car and then noticed the exact same color and model on the roads everywhere? That is because that particular vehicle was picked up by your reticular activating system and it is now on your radar. Attracting money people works the same way. Write down a goal and read it ten times each night right before you go to sleep to help program your subconscious mind. This will help the subconscious law of attraction come into play. You might consider writing down something like this: *"I am a real estate expert and am focused on finding people who have money and who are looking for an honest hardworking man like me to work with."* Write it down and keep flooding your mind with that message throughout the day and especially at night right before you go to sleep. Just like the new car you see everywhere, your subconscious mind will activate your antenna and private lenders will start showing up on your radar. You may want to review the section in Chapter 1 on how and why affirmations work.

Let's say at this point you've saved enough money to do at least one successful deal. Now you need to add some fuel to the fire by finding a private lender. There are "hard-money" lenders whom you may be able to borrow from, but oftentimes, their points, fees, and high interest rates eat into your profits big time. Over the years, we have found that working with private investors is far superior to working with hard-money lenders. Private investors like to get a reasonable return on their money, but they also seem to enjoy the process of helping us reach our goals. Oftentimes they are as passionate as we are about real estate.

PRIVATE LENDER

Story from Mike: *Several years ago my wife and I were in Corpus Christi, Texas, competing in a running event called Beach to Bay Relay. It is a marathon distance race with six runners each running approximately 4.4 miles. While at the post-race party, we struck up a conversation with another married couple, Don and Marylou. I had seen both of them at other running events but had never really talked to them. My wife and I had planned on making the three-hour drive back to San Antonio but Don and Marylou invited us to their home to hang out by their pool and spend the night. Since we had no kids at the time, we said, "Why not?" They cooked us dinner; we drank a few beers and had a really great time.*

A few months later, I got a call from Don. He said he was thinking about buying a weekend lake house up by Canyon Lake, just north of San Antonio. Don knew that I was in the real estate business so he asked if I would help them find a lake house. I found them a nice little weekend getaway, and that was the start of a really good friendship with Don and Marylou. They eventually ended up moving to San Antonio and we all became great friends.

One summer, Don and I went hiking up Mount Royal in Frisco, Colorado. While on the hike, Don and I were talking about my real estate business and also his job as a petroleum engineer. Don was hiking ahead of me and I heard about every other word of the conversation because we were both breathing heavily as we were hiking up a steep part of the mountain. Don said something about investing in oil wells and then I heard $500K. I was thinking, that is fantastic! He is making $500K a year investing in oil wells. Wouldn't that be awesome? Then I thought I hear the word month. I told him to stop in his tracks and said, "Would you please repeat what you just said?" He turned around and said he was making $500K per month. My crazy hiking buddy was making $500K per month? Amazing! That conversation helped stretch my mind and motivated me to take the business to the next level. Don and Marylou live well beneath their means, and they are great role models for being good stewards of their wealth. I have seen them perform many *random acts of kindness with their money and they have had a positive impact on countless lives.*

Over the years, Don and I became really good friends. We started out doing some very small real estate deals and over time he became more and more confident in my ability to consistently make both of us lots of money. Don has loaned me millions of dollars, and both of us have greatly benefited by using our seller-finance strategy.

I realize you probably don't trip across people who make $500K per month every day. The good news is that you don't need to. You can build a very nice portfolio of notes with someone who will lend you enough money to do a couple of deals and there are lots of those guys and gals out there. Focus on becoming an expert and scraping together enough of your own money to do your first deal or two. Then let your subconscious mind help you activate your radar and attract money people.

The main goal with a private lender is to get them to believe in you and write that first check. We don't care if you borrow only $100 and pay them back $120. The goal with a money person is just to get the cash flowing. Once you earn the confidence and trust of the private investor and they believe you are competent, honest, and passionate about the real estate business, they will keep the cash flowing. Remember, the people who *have* the money are more than likely very smart and have worked hard for it. Always make sure they know you appreciate their trust and financial investment and that you will always be a good steward of their money. Take things slowly and let them share in your success. The goal is creating a mutually beneficial relationship built on trust and integrity.

The typical guy or gal who is sitting on a large pile of cash these days does not have a lot of really good options for getting a good return on his or her money. The CD rates at a bank are a joke, and many people do not want to deal with the ups and downs and uncertainty of the stock market. You are providing the private lender with a fantastic opportunity to get a good return on his money and also the satisfaction that he is helping you reach your goals. This is a double win for the money man.

One suggestion on a deal structure that has worked well for us is to have the private lender finance the acquisition of the property and then we pay for 100 percent of the renovation costs. The private lender would have a first lien on the property and know that we are using our own money to fix up the house. Private lenders like to know that you have skin in the game and this arrangement demonstrates to the investor that you are not looking to them for *all* of the money. It shows them that you truly are "partners" on the deal.

The goal with the private lender once again is to get the cash flowing. Pick out very conservative deals at first. Don't go for any home runs. Find a deal you are extremely confident will be a winner even if the profit potential is not huge. In our real estate course, we will teach you how to find deals that will consistently deliver "singles" or "doubles." No home runs are necessary to build massive wealth. Singles are just fine. Demonstrate to the lender your competence and focus on showing them the appreciation and respect they deserve. Take them to lunch on a regular basis and keep them posted on the progress of your projects. A simple phone call or e-mail letting them know the house is ready to go on the market shows your enthusiasm and passion for the business and appreciation and respect for their role in your success.

NOTE BUYERS—HOW TO FIND THEM

Let's assume you have the private lender piece of the puzzle covered. Remember, you can build significant wealth with our business model by having a private lender loan you just enough money to do *one deal.* How? By getting one or two of the other key pieces of the puzzle in place. We are talking about finding note buyers to purchase your notes and also banks to help you build your own portfolio of notes. We will tackle note buyers first, but let's review why this business model is so superior to traditional house flipping.

With traditional house flipping, basically you have created a job. Even if you have access to lots of money and are really good at what you do, it's a job and you have to work very hard to earn your money. The vision of the owner-finance model is to get your money working hard for YOU. We have done hundreds of traditional flips and hundreds of owner-finance transactions and the owner-finance model is superior…period. Quite simply, owner financing homes is easier! You are bringing so much value by offering owner-financing terms that you don't have to deal with many of the issues associated with traditional house flipping. You don't have to negotiate on price or interest rate. You can sell the home with a minimal renovation and you don't have to pay a full 6 percent commission to a Realtor, which will eat up a good portion of your profit.

Let's assume that you studied this book, followed the steps, and created a quality real estate note. Now you have a problem you need to solve. Most of your money is tied up in that real estate note and in order to realize your profit immediately, you need to sell your note! If you Google *note buyers*, you will find a huge list of people who say they want to buy your note. This is fantastic, right? Wrong! What you will find is that they are looking to *steal* your note. Generally speaking, most note buyers who advertise online and through direct mail want to buy your note at a steep discount. Let's say you have a note for $75,000. They may offer you $40K to $50K if you are lucky. Our advice is to not waste your time talking to "note buyers" and "note brokers" who advertise online. Instead, focus your energy on finding *private* note buyers who you can educate on your business model and show them how you can deliver double-digit returns and steady monthly income to them. This is exactly what the majority of retired folks are looking for. Steady, monthly income.

So, how do you find private note buyers? Start with the older crowd. Think of yourself as a problem solver. What problem do older people have? They are at an age where they are either retired or soon-to-be retired and trying to live off of the money they saved during their working years. In today's world, many people are working well into their seventies simply because they cannot live off of the income of their nest egg. Your real estate note may be the perfect solution to their problem! I can tell you story after story about retired folks who were in a desperate situation and we have helped "rescue" their retirement. Look at the limited options that a typical sixty-five-year-old has. They can walk into a bank and get paid 1 to 2 percent from a CD if they are lucky, or they can invest in the stock market and pray we don't have another financial meltdown during their golden years. You must *believe* that you have the perfect solution to their problem. How about being able to offer them approximately five times what they can get at a bank! If you follow the steps in this book and do a good job underwriting, you will have the perfect solution to their problem!

EDUCATING A NOTE BUYER

The key points that we address with prospective note buyers to educate them on the investment opportunity of owning notes are the following:

1. The real estate note is secured by a first lien.
2. A substantial down payment was collected at the time of closing and the person making the payment is NOT a tenant. They OWN the house and have skin in the game. There is no fixing toilets when you owner finance.
3. The borrowers' taxes and insurance are escrowed monthly.
4. The mortgage payments to note buyers are wired to their account monthly.
5. If the borrower refinances or sells the home, the remaining loan balance gets paid to the note buyer.
6. Explain the due diligence you did during the underwriting process to verify the buyers' income and prior rental history.
7. Show them a copy of the settlement statement from the title company verifying the down payment, escrow account, proof of property, and title insurance.
8. Show them several pictures of the house that showcase the work that you did to the property during the renovation process.

9. Regarding the legal process of purchasing a note, there is a document called "Transfer of Note and Liens," which gets signed, notarized, and recorded at the county courthouse. Also, the original real estate note gets endorsed to the note buyer. There are samples of these documents on our website, TheNoteFactory.com.
10. Let them know that your intent is to provide them with passive streams of income and if there is ever a disruption to the income stream, you have the expertise to get it back on track quickly.

RISK VS. REWARD

The question about a potential foreclosure almost always comes up. It has been our experience that a foreclosure is not necessarily a bad thing. The times we have had to foreclose or take a "deed in lieu" of foreclosure, we have been able to remarket the property very quickly, usually within sixty to ninety days, AND our note buyers have made money every time! Other than the hassle factor, a foreclosure is not a big deal. If you own a stock and it plummets all you can do is hope and pray that it goes up again someday. If a homeowner quits paying their mortgage, you can roll up your sleeves and quickly do something about it and get your income stream back on track. When talking to note buyers, we spend a lot of time on this one specific point. The control over the investment is *huge*. Also, each state has a unique foreclosure process. In Texas, we have a nonjudicial process. This is why many out-of-state buyers like Texas real estate notes. Be sure to check with a local real estate attorney so that you understand the foreclosure process in your state.

All investments come with some degree of risk and it is your job to educate the prospective note buyer and get them comfortable with the risks associated with owning a real estate note. This may sound like a daunting task at first, but once you sell that first note, it will get much easier to sell notes two, three, and four. By the way, if you have another job or income stream and don't *have* to sell your notes to realize your profit, you can start working with a bank to build your own portfolio of notes. Also, depending on how deep the pockets are on your private lender, they may be the perfect first-note buyer.

We mentioned that the older crowd is a good place to start, but note buyers are basically anyone with money. If they have money, they can buy notes. This can be relatives, friends, parents, neighbors, etc. Anyone who has money, whether it is in a retirement account or stuffed under a mattress, can potentially be a note buyer.

Start small. Start with just "pitching" your friends and relatives. Practice the art of trying to educate and persuade someone to consider making real estate notes part of their investment strategy. One lesson you will need to learn is patience and this is one of the hardest things when you are anxious to sell your note. If you try to "close the deal" in one meeting you will rarely get someone to commit. Also, do not underestimate the contagious effect of being enthusiastic about real estate notes.

> ***"Enthusiasm is a state of mind. It inspires action and is the most contagious of all emotions.***
>
> ***"Enthusiasm is a combination of mental and physical energy which is seldom found in an ailing body. It thrives best where sound physical health abounds. Sound health begins with the development and maintenance of health consciousness, just as economic success begins with prosperity consciousness."***
>
> —*NAPOLEON HILL*

Here is a sample dialogue to move the note selling process along in the right direction:

Potential Note Buyer: What do you do for a living John?

You: I create and sell real estate notes to private investors. My notes generally pay double-digit returns, and I do all of the note servicing. Basically I help people create long-term streams of passive income.

Potential Note Buyer: Interesting. So how does it work?

You: I purchase homes, renovate them, and find quality buyers who put down a significant down payment. Then I sell those mortgages or "real estate notes" to private investors like you.

Potential Note Buyer: So I am assuming that most of your note buyers have lots of money?

You: Not really. Typically the notes I create are in the $60K-to-$80K range and there is no minimum on the number of notes you need to buy. I often sell one note at a time. Also, many people use their retirement accounts to purchase the notes.

Potential Note Buyer: Very interesting, John.

You: So, did you see the Cowboys game last night? [Intentionally change the subject after this brief dialogue. You do not want to overwhelm them with information in the first meeting. Just let the conversation marinate in their mind. It takes time for everything you just said to resonate with the prospect. If he or she is interested, and believe me many people are interested in passive double-digit returns, he will make the next move and start asking you more questions.]

If the prospect does not bring up the subject again or does not call you in the next week or so, circle back with them and bring up the subject of notes again. The note investment education process is just that: a process. It often takes multiple conversations to finally get a prospect to understand the business model enough to want to take a serious look.

Once you have someone who wants to take a serious look at real estate notes, schedule a meeting with them and carefully go through the entire process of what you do. Slowly go over each step of the process and explain the steps that you took to create the real estate note. Drive them by the property if they would like to see it. Once again, we have sold hundreds of notes and every time we get a new note buyer, it is the education of the process that finally gets them comfortable with purchasing the note. Take it slow and be sure to listen carefully to their questions. In our education course, we will provide you with a sample note binder and actually walk you through exactly what to say and how to present the paperwork associated with a real estate note sale.

Birds of a feather flock together. Once you get your first note sold, your note buyer will hopefully tell his friends that he is getting double-digit returns and you will start getting referrals. Ninety percent of the clients who buy our notes come from referrals. The toughest note to sell is the first one. Focus on bringing a first-class home to the marketplace and finding a quality buyer who has a significant down payment. Then you *will* find a note buyer who appreciates the value and stream of income you have created.

We hope you recognize the common theme on working with all money people: trust, integrity, value, and relationship. There are no shortcuts to success, so don't try to take one. You need to work hard to build all of these relationships and work on becoming the absolute best version of yourself. Become the person who money people *want* to deal with. Also, don't forget to practice the law of reciprocity. The psychological law of reciprocity says, *If you are kind to others, they will reciprocate and be kind to you.* When you look for every opportunity to do and say things that have a positive impact on your money people, you will be astonished by their response. We always look for opportunities to do something special for our private investors and bankers. Never turn down an opportunity to help a millionaire.

BANKING RELATIONSHIPS

As we begin our discussion on banking relationships, let's start by looking at some numbers on a typical real estate note that has been created using our system. We have educated many people on our business model and many folks have decided that it was just easier to purchase notes from us instead of trying to do it themselves. Either way you go, we want you to understand how you can leverage your notes with a banking relationship.

Purchase Price of Home: $50,000
Renovation Costs: $15,000
Total Investment: $65,000
Sales Price of the Home: $85,000
Down Payment Received: $10,000
Note Created: $75,000

If you created this note, your total investment after you received the down payment is $55,000 ($65K minus the down payment you received of $10K equals 55K). We have found that banks have been willing to lend 75 to 80 percent of the note value. If we take 75 percent of the $75,000 note, this means the bank will lend you $56,250. Once again, your total investment after receiving your down payment was only $55K! You now have 100 percent of your working capital back and you can do it again and again and again! Are you starting to get the picture? Even if you only have enough money to do one deal, you can slowly build up a significant pool of notes and start building massive wealth!

Let's take a look at the following numbers so that you understand the cash flow on a typical deal:

Payment on a $75,000 Loan Amortized for 25 Years at 11.9 Percent: $784.38
Payment to Bank ($56,250 Financed for 10 Years at 6 Percent): $624.49
Positive Cash Flow: $159.89
Amount Owed to Bank After 10 Years: $0
Amount Owed by Borrower After 10 Years: $65,575.03

If this example really sinks in, you may end up losing some sleep tonight. After you pay off the bank, you are still owed $65,575.03! Remember, this was a twenty-five-year note and you paid the bank off in ten years or hopefully less. This means that the borrower still owes you fifteen more years of payments at $784.38 per month. If they pay as scheduled, you will receive $141,188.40 after the bank is paid off (180 payments remaining after the bank is paid off times the monthly payment of $784.38). By the way, we used twenty-five-year financing instead of thirty because that is the way we teach it in our courses. We have found that note buyers prefer notes shorter than thirty years so we currently finance most of our homes for ten to twenty-five years. Be sure to consult with your CPA to discuss the cash flow and income tax ramifications while building your note portfolio. We have found that building a portfolio of notes with a combination of ten- and fifteen-year financing with the bank has created the cash flow needed to pay down the debt at an accelerated pace and also service the tax liability.

If you choose to purchase notes from us and not go through all of the work to produce the notes yourself, you can still work with banks. We have helped many people build their own portfolio without ever leaving their desk.

Regarding tips for working with bankers, here are a few things that may help:

1. It is a wise decision to obtain a credit report on yourself before you apply for credit. If you discover any inaccuracies or problems, you can correct them before any damage to your loan application has occurred. If you can, find out which credit reporting company your prospective lender uses and request a report from that company.
2. Keep in mind that to stay in business banks need to make loans. Do not be afraid to ask for one. That is what the loan officer wants you to do. To increase your chances of getting a loan, look for a bank that does a lot of real estate lending and is familiar with notes.

3. Seek out banks that are active in small-business financing. As an entrepreneur, make sure that you are thoroughly prepared when you go to your banker's office to request a loan. You need to show your banker that a loan to you is a low-risk proposition. Have on hand a completed loan application and a current financial statement.
4. Learn to anticipate every question that he or she has. Remember, the combination of information and preparation is the most powerful negotiating tool in the world. A confident and thoroughly prepared borrower is much more likely to have his or her loan approved than a borrower who does not know the answer to some of the basic questions a banker may ask.
5. Show your banker exactly how the cash flow will work on a typical note. Point out to the banker your confidence in the borrower and point out the significant down payment that the borrower paid.
6. For this type of financing and so you can sleep at night, request a fixed interest rate for as long of a term as possible.
7. Dress professionally for the interview. This is a business transaction, so treat it as such.
8. Do not stretch the truth in your loan application. Broad, unsubstantiated statements should be avoided. The lender can easily check many of the facts on your application. If you cannot support statements with solid data, then don't make them.
9. Be sure all your documents are neat, legible, and organized in a cohesive and attractive manner. Don't forget to include a cover letter.
10. Do not push the loan officer for a decision. Most loan officers have to go to a loan committee, so do not look or act overly anxious.
11. Be confident. An attitude of confidence enhances your chance of getting the loan. Show that you can make a success out of the money that the bank will lend to you. Visualize in your mind the positive results of your bank application. Jim Rohn used to tell a story about the first banker who ever took a chance on him. He believes what pushed the banker over the edge to give him the loan was the fact that Jim said something like this: "When I become rich and famous someday, I am

going to tell everyone you were the banker that first believed in me." Jim really believed that is what helped persuade the banker to make the loan. You might just want to try that one!

12. Ask someone to give you a good referral. Before you decide to approach a bank directly, find an associate, friend, or acquaintance who is in good standing with the bank to give you a good referral. Bankers tend to deal more favorably with those who were referred to them by their best customers.
13. Remember that the first loan is usually the hardest to get. Bankers prefer to lend money to borrowers who have borrowed at least once and have paid back at least one loan on time. They are not venture capitalists, who make high-risk loans regardless of the profit prospects of your business. Bankers prefer to lend to low-risk ventures and lending 75 or 80 percent of the note value is a low-risk loan for a bank.
14. Don't come in with too small of a vision. Even if you are going to slowly build notes one at a time, we would recommend approaching the banker with a vision of building up a large pool of notes over time.

We would be remiss if we did not implore you to make sure that you are not overextending yourself. Make sure you have the cash reserves to make payments to the bank even if your borrower stops making *their* payments. Remember, the key to moving forward with confidence is being diligent during the underwriting process and making sure that you find a well-qualified buyer who makes a significant down payment. We have experienced less than a 5 percent default rate since our inception, and the great news is that every time we have had a default, we ended up with an increased return for our note holders.

One other suggestion that has worked well for us when presenting our vision to a bank is providing them with an executive summary. An executive summary is a short document used in business to summarize a proposal so that everyone can quickly get the big picture of the business plan. Here is an example of an executive summary:

EXECUTIVE SUMMARY

opportunity

We are producing quality first lien real estate notes in Texas. Taxes and insurance are escrowed on all notes and we use a third-party mortgage company to produce our loan documents to ensure compliance with all Dodd-Frank rules and regulations. At this time we have a credit line to "warehouse" about 20 percent of our annual note volume. Currently, 80 percent of the notes being created are being sold to private investors or institutional note buyers. We want to work with your bank and move toward a business model that would allow us to hold the majority of our note production for the next five years.

strategy

Purchase distressed properties at a discount, professionally renovate the homes, and sell them to the hardworking families of our community at a reasonable market value. The typical borrower is actively employed with family ties to the neighborhood. Target properties are two to four bedrooms, one to two baths in well-established neighborhoods. The typical note has a fifteen to thirty year amortization term with an interest rate of 9.9 percent to 11.9 percent. Borrowers typically pay 10 percent down and $750 to $1,000 per month, which includes taxes and insurance. These monthly payments are consistent with the cost to rent a home in similar areas.

problem

By having to sell off 80 percent of the current note production, we are leaving a huge amount of money on the table since we are not going to collect and benefit from those streams of income.

solution

Find a lending partner that will allow us to warehouse our current annual note volume for the next five years.

being the "Note Factory" gives us a huge advantage.
Most note portfolio managers or institutional note buyers make their living off the positive cash flow. We have the acquisition, renovation, and sales team in place to actually create and service our own notes. Since we are The Note Factory, we are able to make a profit when we sell a home, thus allowing us to **use the monthly cash flow to pay down the debt**.

performance
Our Proprietary Character Underwriting System has produced a default rate of about 5 percent since inception and results continue to improve. Every loan default has resulted in a profitable transaction and a quick turnaround time to get the stream of income back on track. The bottom line is that the market is extremely liquid and the demand for these homes is very strong. If we ever have a nonperforming note as collateral for the bank, we replace it with a performing note.

why now
Texas is booming and values are rising. We are a leader in the marketplace and we have an expert team in place and a proven track record. The demand for "seller financing" in the community is huge. We want to keep the profits generated from our business model in Texas and not discount our notes to institutional out-of-state buyers.

• • •

We have used this Executive Summary format with all of our banking relationships, and guess what? It works! All bankers like a simple one-page summary that they can show to the loan committee.

Wow, you made it this far! Way to go! The final chapter will help encourage you to take some concrete action steps that will get you on the road to building wealth.

ERIK AND MIKE'S BOTTOM LINE:
Nothing replaces the real-life experience of scraping together enough of your own money to do your first real estate transaction. After you do your first one, attracting investors and working with banks will get much easier.

"Everyone holds his fortune in his own hands, like a sculptor the raw material he will fashion into a figure. But it's the same with that type of artistic activity as with all others: We are merely born with the capability to do it. The skill to mold the material into what we want must be learned and attentively cultivated."

—Johann Wolfgang von Goethe

11

WHAT NOW?

We would like to thank you for taking the time to read our story. The information and stories presented have been developed from many years of experience, sweat, and hard work. We have extracted and concentrated our most valuable insights and knowledge about the business with the goal of passing it on to you. However, you have only taken the first steps on your journey to become successful in the real estate note business. Now you must put your knowledge into *action*. There are three paths of action that we encourage you to take daily in order to achieve your goal of becoming a million-dollar investor.

SHARPENING THE SAW

The first path of action that we encourage you to pursue is the persistent daily acquisition of more knowledge. We like to call this "sharpening the saw." You must "sharpen the saw" daily to stay on top of a specific topic or field. If you want to be an expert in something it is in your best interest to read every book, attend every seminar, and take all the courses you can relating to your area of focus. A past mentor of ours once said, "If you think education is expensive, try ignorance."

Set aside time every day to become an expert and exercise your mind. Whether you choose real estate notes as your path to wealth or another road, invest the time to become an expert. Our firm belief in the power of education is the reason we are now dedicating large amounts of our time to teaching others the philosophies and skills we have acquired and refined over the years. When you are persistent in your pursuit of expertise in a single subject, the knowledge you acquire over time can be astounding. Becoming an expert and helping others reach their goals is a very rewarding experience.

BABY STEPS

The second path that we encourage you to pursue is the path of taking small action steps every day. We encourage you to look at the accumulation of your skills and knowledge as a journey. Every journey begins with one small step forward in the right direction. What step can you take *right now* to begin the path to building your own massive stream of income? Take the first step *now*. Get out a piece of paper and write down your goals, sign up for a course, read the first chapter of another real estate book, pick up the phone and make a call about a property, whatever you do, *start now*. Take one small action to gain momentum and take the first step on your journey. The power of a little momentum in the right direction can change the course of your life!

Many people fail to make it past the first step because they look at the task as one major obstacle that needs to be overcome immediately. Their limiting beliefs make the task as a whole overwhelming and they give up without ever taking the first step. Change the way you look at the task by viewing it as a journey with the understanding that you will take small persistent baby steps toward your goal each day. Remember, direction is the key. Not destination. Focus on going in the right direction and someday soon you will arrive.

> ***"There are two kinds of failure. The first comes from never trying out your ideas because you are afraid, or because you are waiting for the perfect time. This kind of failure you can never learn from, and such timidity will destroy you. The second kind comes from a bold and venturesome spirit. If you fail in this way, the hit that you take to your reputation is greatly outweighed by what you learn. Repeated***

> ***failure will toughen your spirit and show you with absolute clarity how things must be done."***
>
> —*ROBERT GREENE*

WALK IN SOMEONE'S FOOTSTEPS

The third path of action, and perhaps the most critical, is to find a mentor to help guide you on your path. Whether it be meeting with someone weekly who is in the same business or hiring a seasoned pro, finding someone who has already walked the path that you want to walk is invaluable. Oftentimes, mentors can provide you with firsthand experience of their mistakes, learning curves, and hiccups that they encountered on their wealth journey. They may be able to condense and communicate years of experience into one simple conversation. That one conversation might save you five years of headaches! It is in your best interest to surround yourself with like-minded individuals and find an experienced mentor.

> ***"The best way a mentor can prepare another leader is to expose him or her to other great people."***
>
> —*JOHN C. MAXWELL*

Like fists punching the same spot on a punching bag over time, the long-term effects of daily learning, daily action, and aligning yourself with a mentor will eventually begin to compound. When you feel that you have successfully integrated these three daily pursuits into your schedule, it is time to begin quantifying them and tracking your progress. This is done with goal setting.

GOAL SETTING

> ***"Setting your goals is the first step to turning the invisible into the visible."***
>
> —*TONY ROBBINS*

Goals and philosophy are your sail, and your road to wealth is your boat. Take the time to visualize your future and what you want it to look like in five or ten years. Where do you want to live? Who do you want in your life? What would a perfect day look like for you? Develop a compelling vision of the future and embed it into your brain. Try to visualize the images as clearly as possible. The more clear these images are, the more they will serve you. These visions of your future are the fuel that will power you during your journey. Your visions are the *why* behind the tedious steps that you must take each day. When the *why* becomes clear, you will have "fuel" to be persistent in carrying out the daily actions needed to achieve your vision. Your *why* will be the wind in your sail. It will sustain you in difficult times, it will get you out of bed at 5:00 a.m. and it will drive you to work one more hour late into the night. If you know *exactly why* you are taking the actions, the thoughts of doubt that creep into your mind will be overcome by a stronger, more powerful vision of your future.

Our *why* that pulled us through the tough times during the writing of this book was this: We held on to a clear vision of helping other investors, just like you, do their first deal and start on the path to their own personal wealth journey. That is a powerful vision and it provided us with the fuel to complete this project and focus more of our energy on building an education course to accomplish our goal of helping others build wealth. Our course can be found on our website TheNoteFactory.com

The further you walk down a path to achieve a goal, the clearer your surroundings become. At first you might feel like you are walking down a foggy path in the forest, only able to see one foot in front of you. However, if you remain persistent, momentum will slowly build and the clarity of the final outcome will increase exponentially. If you are disciplined and focused and have a clear vision of *why*, you will eventually produce phenomenal results.

Transcribing your goals from your imagination to a sheet of paper is the key first step in goal setting. When you bring an invisible goal in your head into the physical world with writing, you are doing something incredibly powerful. You are making the invisible visible, you are making something intangible tangible. When you write down your goals you are 10 times more likely to act on them and accomplish them. *Not* writing down your goals is like planting an acorn and then never giving it enough water or sunlight to grow. The key to successful goal setting is to take the time to fully decide what you really want in life and to write it down. If you don't do this, thoughts and dreams just float around in your brain as ambiguous, unclear, unorganized, "wants" as opposed to a clear, calculated, well-thought-out goals.

Organize your goals into four different key areas of your life: health, family, financial, and spiritual. As you write your goals, try to put them into the most appropriate category. Setting goals is like any other skill; it takes practice. See if you can come up with 10 goals in each key area of your life and list at least one action step you can take immediately to get some momentum going. Also write a short *why* next to each goal. There are no wrong answers here. We ask *why* because sometimes a goal just isn't worth going after. Don't get hung up on doing this perfectly. If you don't like a goal, cross it out. If you don't like the whole list, tear it up and start over. Goal setting is a never-ending and fluid process.

After you get your list of goals completed, take a look at each one of them individually and ask yourself the following questions: *How many years do I think it will take to reach that goal?* Give it your best shot and put either a one, three, five, or ten in the blank. This will help you make sure that you have a good balance of short-term and longer-term goals. Use a 1 for all goals that should take one year or less. If all of your goals have a 1 on them, you need to stretch your brain and learn how to look further down the road and set some longer-term goals.

Here is a sample of a few health goals and financial goals to help you get the wheels turning:

HEALTH GOALS:
Goal: Lose ten pounds by June first. (1)
Action step: Throw all of the soda away today and commit to drinking only water.

Why: I will be going to my cousin's wedding in June and want everyone to tell me how great I look!
Goal: Run my first 10K by September first (1)
Action step: Print off a training program from the Internet and tape it to my bathroom mirror and buy a new pair of running shoes.
Why: That cute girl at the country club loves to run and I want to get into shape so I can run with her.

Goal: Complete an Ironman triathlon. (3)
Action step: Buy a book about triathlons on Amazon and sign up for swimming lessons.
Why: Give my life a sense of adventure and it will motivate me to reach for larger goals.

Goal: Climb all of the fifty-three mountains in Colorado above 14,000 feet (fourteeners). (10)
Action Step: Schedule a ten-day vacation and book the flight and pick out my first five mountains to climb during that time.
Why: It will motivate me to live a healthy lifestyle and allow me to consistently enjoy nature with friends and family.

FINANCIAL GOALS:
Goal: Save up a total of $100,000 (3)
Action step: Call the payroll department and ask them to start deducting 20 percent out of my check each month and depositing it directly into my savings account.
Why: I want to be able to have some working capital of my own when I start working with private lenders.

Goal: Find three possible people who might consider lending me money once I become an expert in the real estate business. (1)
Action step: Make a list of everyone I know who might be a possible private lender.

Why: Building relationships with these key people will help me when I approach them after I do my first successful transaction on my own.

Goal: Pay off my home. (10)
Action step: Call the mortgage company and have them deduct an extra $200 each month from my checking account to be applied to principal.
Why: When I retire my house will almost be paid for and I will have plenty of money to travel.

Goal: Create $300,000 in passive annual income. (10)
Action step: Break out my calculator and start figuring out how many notes I will need to create over the next decade.
Why: I can live my retirement years in style and help out other family members with my income.

Once you get into the habit of knocking out things on your list, it will create momentum and motivate you to set larger and longer-term goals.

WARNING: This habit can become addicting and cause you to have extreme success in all areas of your life!

FIND THE RIGHT WALL

After you have clearly defined, organized, and recorded your goals and discovered the *why* behind them, the next step is to develop a well-thought-out plan to achieve them. This is the *how*. Begin by developing a vision for your long-term wealth journey and realize that sometimes identifying exactly what you *don't want* can be just as valuable as finding out what you *do want* in life.

Do you want to lean your ladder on the wall of a corporation with a measly company-issued 401(k) and end up with a dwindling Social Security check and a gold watch? Do you want to continue to be a slave to your clients and bosses who underappreciate you? You may be the hardest working and most honest person on the planet, but if your ladder is leaning against the wrong wall, it will lead to an unfulfilling and disappointing end.

Be smart with your wealth plan. Choose a path that you are confident will get you there. Real estate investing has created more millionaires than any other vehicle, and our real estate note model is one of the best paths available. Becoming wealthy is a worthwhile goal. Don't sell yourself short. Go for it. It does take some time to get there, but time is going to go by either way. You might as well start the journey today.

GOALS TO PRIORITIES—CONTROL YOUR STATE OF MIND

As you begin your wealth journey, there will be moments when you have to decide what takes priority. Your goals or the distractions of daily life. You must be able to prioritize and control your state of mind so you can decipher what is most important to you. Having the state of mind to remain focused and persistent is a skill that must be cultivated on a daily basis. When you are in the process of developing and working on your goals it is crucial that you are aware of subtle thoughts that are entering your mind. Oftentimes our minds are preprogrammed to feed us negative and hypercritical thoughts. You must develop a sense of awareness for identifying when you are being fed these negative thoughts, which create limiting beliefs. By simply being aware of these thoughts you will begin to have the power to overcome them.

When you are starting your journey, the idea of making $10,000 a month might sound attainable, but what about the idea of making $100,000 a month? Your initial subconscious response might be "impossible." Allowing yourself to accept this limiting belief as truth will paralyze you from achieving big goals. The response triggered by your brain might be derived from your reference of other people's salary or your own experience with making money. It is a false parameter that you cannot accept as truth. Once you become aware of your limiting beliefs, you can overcome them and open up a world with limitless possibilities.

MASTERY

> ***"The key then to attaining this higher level of intelligence is to make our years of study qualitatively rich. We don't simply absorb information—we internalize it and make it our own by finding some way to put this knowledge to practical use."***
>
> **—*Robert Greene***

When we asked you the question at the beginning of this chapter "What Now?" we wanted to provide you with a series of step-by-step logical actions that would guide you on your path to achieving your goals. Many people will take *some* action and get *some* results. Some results are good, but we don't want you to settle for "average" in any area of your life. We want to challenge you to go beyond average—way beyond average.

Stretch yourself to go beyond your expectations. Allocate your highest degree of focus and commitment to all areas of your life. Your passion and excitement to master all areas is in the details. You can't fake success. What good is a million dollars if you don't have the health or loved ones to enjoy it with? Being successful is a lot more than the amount of money in your bank account. It is living a well-balanced and meaningful life with the ones you love.

Everyone will read this book differently. Although we all can read the same book, we will not all read the same thing. This book was written to give you ideas and guidance. We did not intend for this to be a step-by-step instruction book on how to create and sell real estate notes. We wanted it to be more about the philosophies needed to create a good real estate business and how and why you should build one—something with a strong foundation, something that will last forever. That is what we want for you. Something you can be proud of. A business that was built out of goodness and one that gives back to, not only takes from, the community that supports it. We are confident that if you follow this book, you, too, can have a successful business as well as life. Many of the philosophies we describe correlate both to business and life. Never build one and not the other, for to be truly successful, you must build them together.

ERIK AND MIKE'S BOTTOM LINE:

Take action *now* and never underestimate the power of momentum. Invest time to set your goals and display them where you can review them daily. Do this for thirty days and you will probably end up doing it for a lifetime.

12

HOW TO USE A FINANCIAL CALCULATOR

The ***How to Use a Financial Calculator*** course can be found by visiting www.TheNoteFactory.com and clicking on the link. Type the word ***book*** as the password to access this course for ***free***.

It is imperative that you become familiar with how to use a financial calculator when dealing with real estate investing and especially when creating, buying, or selling real estate notes.

The HP 12C can be very intimidating at first, but once you understand the basics, it is fairly simple to use. They even have an app for your iPhone.

Once you learn how to use the HP 12C, you will be able to solve for payment, interest, return, payoff, future value, ROI, plus much, much more.

Please take the time to watch the in-depth video online that we have created. This video will walk you through the entire process with step-by-step instructions with pictures.

"If you have a dream, you can spend a lifetime studying, planning, and getting ready for it. What you should be doing is getting started."

-Drew Houston

13

FINAL THOUGHTS

This book was intended to be more than a practical guide for building a thriving real estate note portfolio. We wanted to encourage you through our stories, quotes, number crunching, philosophies, and practical real estate advice. We are just a couple of average guys who held on tightly to the success principles of integrity, hard work, and perseverance. It has been an honor to share what we have learned. We hope and pray that you will have an amazing and successful wealth journey.

As we end our time together and as a final farewell, we would be remiss if we did not implore you to constantly seek wisdom throughout your life. Discovering the truths and acting in accordance with those truths is the key to a successful business and life.

The definition of *wisdom* is "having experience, knowledge, and good judgment; the quality of being wise." As the following quote by Marcel Proust teaches us, wisdom must be discovered throughout your life's journey. Studying proverbs is a great way to get some insight into some of the truths that were discovered by some of the wisest men who ever lived.

> ***"We are not provided with wisdom, we must discover it for ourselves, after a journey through the wilderness which no one else can take for us, and effort which no one can spare us."***
>
> —*Marcel Proust*

The definition of a *proverb* is "a short saying that is widely used to express an obvious truth." Once you discover the truths in life, you will be able to apply good judgment and slowly but surely acquire wisdom. Acquiring wisdom is a worthwhile goal and more valuable than gold or silver. When you feel that you need a course correction in life, it is always helpful to fill your mind with some fundamental truths to help keep you on track. Take the time to read proverbs in the Bible, and may God bless you and all of the people you love and care about.

The proverb we started the company with:

Proverbs 3: 5–6
Trust in the Lord with all your heart
and lean not on your own understanding;
in all your ways submit to him,
and he will make your paths straight.

Thank you,

Mike Arch
Erik Saengerhausen

About the authors

Erik Saengerhausen has been an entrepreneur since the age of twenty and is the cofounder of The Note Factory. He is well-respected in the real estate investment community and considered one of the foremost experts at the seller-finance business model.

Erik is married to his wife, Brittany, and they have two sons, Colton, age eight, and Parker, age two. Erik enjoys boating, fishing, and playing basketball and tennis. He lives in a lake community in south Texas.

Mike Arch has been an entrepreneur for thirty years and is the cofounder of The Note Factory. He has been involved in hundreds of real estate transactions and is passionate about helping others reach their personal and financial goals.

Mike is married to Kimberly, and they have two daughters, Delaney and Macy, ages eleven and eight. Mike enjoys running, swimming, biking, hiking, and playing tennis with his wife. Mike is actively involved in his community and church and enjoys spending as much time as possible with his family.

39991752R00136

Made in the USA
Middletown, DE
30 January 2017